Come With Me to Kathmandu draws together the moving stories of twelve Nepali women from extremely diverse backgrounds and social classes, yet unifies them all under one umbrella – faith in Jesus Christ. The beauty demonstrated for the reader in *Come with Me* is that Christ does not instantaneously solve every life problem; rather, he gradually takes hopeless circumstances and people – like many troubled women in Nepal – and through faith begins to bring healing to body, mind, emotions, and soul.

Anna Townsend writes as a woman who has not only heard these gripping stories first-hand, but has also experienced the life and culture in which these stories emerged. Those who have lived in Nepal will appreciate the familiar flavours and cultural elements drawn out, and those who have not yet visited the colourful Himalayan country will be challenged by both the needs and courage found there.

Jim Barron, pastor at Kathmandu International
Christian Congregation

A must-read for anyone wanting to understand more of the situation, status and cultural treatment of women in Nepal, even today in the twenty-first century. You will find stories of the amazing courage, inner strength and endurance that these women show in facing incredibly difficult situations, including the added hardship and stigma of contracting leprosy. I learnt new things about the negative, oppressive, unjust culture towards women in Nepal that I hadn't known before. An inspiring, moving book that challenges us to pray for and work for justice and change for all the women of Nepal.

Peter Bisset, missionary with International
Nepal Fellowship for 35 years

These are stories that are remarkable from beginning to end, yet they could easily have remained hidden and been forgotten about.

These twelve women are astonishing and unique. At the same time, their stories represent so many girls and women in Nepal, as they give insight into many of the hardships they encounter in this country; from domestic violence, traff the practice of *chhaupadi*, mental health issues, polygamy, son-preference, and documentation struggles, to financial dependency in abusive relationships. What makes the deepest impression though, is the women's courage and hope sparked by their Christian faith. This leaves me with hope for anyone and for Nepal.

Liv Wendel, midwife with United Mission to
Nepal serving in Okhaldhunga

For those who want to learn something of the reality of life in Nepal, but perhaps think that they don't have the courage or opportunity to travel, this book is for you! Anna is both a gentle guide and an inspiration to do what we can, where we are, and with what we have to hand.

Anna's beautiful storytelling somehow makes the reader feel safe and treasured just as she values and loves each of these beautiful women whose stories she tells. *Come With Me to Kathmandu* is an invitation to accompany, to listen, to open your heart and to respond.

Anna has a light and airy persona, she is gentle and fun and through the pages of this book the reader will discover her love for the people of Nepal, and her courage in helping women whose lives have been tragically scarred. She has literally walked through the bustling dusty noise of Kathmandu to sit under the roofs of these women. With the help of Saru, her colleague and friend, she has listened, observed, cried and cared. In fact, the roofs under which these women shared their stories have been provided by the very charity that Anna set up.

This book shouts for those who have no voice. This book proclaims the transforming love and power of Christ Jesus to rescue and heal the downtrodden. This book calls out compassion and hope and tells the reader that God can do immeasurably more than we can imagine if we dare to answer his call.

Carole Darling, served with Interserve and
United Mission to Nepal 2002–2009

Anna connects you to Nepal through heartfelt stories and historical facts, igniting a call to action to bring light to the darkest of areas. She shows how a step of faith can impact the lives of many.

Anna captures the stories of women who represent a variety of backgrounds with the common thread of needing an advocate for justice and extension of mercy. May we all live out our lives as Micah 6:8 instructs.

Grab a cup of tea and immerse yourself in a cultural journey through the lives of vulnerable women who have risen up past darkness through the powerful light given by Jesus Christ.

Mary Lou Sorensen, director at Veritacore Nepal

Read this book. It will transport you to an intersection, where you'll join the collective journey of a British woman with a mission, a dozen Nepali ladies with the audacity to keep climbing, and God. On the way, you'll experience something of the history, culture, religions, exasperations and joys of this Himalayan land. All in all – a trip to lift your heart.

Mark and Deirdre Zimmerman, long-term medical missionaries in Nepal

Come With Me to Kathmandu

12 powerful stories of women's courageous faith in Nepal

Anna Townsend

Authentic

First published 2023 by Authentic Media Limited,
PO Box 6326, Bletchley, Milton Keynes, MK1 9GG.
authenticmedia.co.uk

British Library Cataloguing in Publication Data
A catalogue record for this book is available from the British Library.
ISBN: 978-1-78893-248-6
978-1-78893-249-3 (e-book)

Cover design by Jennifer Burrell, Fresh Vision Design
Printed and bound by Micropress Printers Ltd, Southwold, IP18 6SZ

I wish to dedicate this book to all the women who have graciously shared their stories with me. Your strength astonishes me, and your faith is an inspiration.

Foreword

The manuscript for Anna Townsend's book, *Come With Me to Kathmandu*, came into my hands when Authentic Media, Anna's publisher, approached me to write a foreword. Our connection is Kathmandu, that amazing city in which I lived from the mid-70s and through the 80s, and because of that I was immediately interested in what Anna had written.

Although we have both lived in Kathmandu, the city I lived in and the one Anna experienced are almost incomparable. Mine was an old, rustic, picturesque city which had a population of around 180,000 when I first arrived. It was a city which had a feel of a large town rather than one similar to the many other large, heavily populated cities across South Asia. Mine was one of looking out at open rice fields across the surrounding valley and at crystal clear views of the snow-capped Himalayan mountains beyond.

Anna's Kathmandu could not be more different. As people have migrated from rural areas it has become a city which now has a population of almost 3 million inhabitants, who are squeezed into every available piece of concrete as buildings have been erected on every piece of land across the valley. The majestic snow-covered mountains are almost invisible now as they are hidden behind a heavy veil of thick pollution emanating from the fumes of endless streams of traffic and smoke from wood fires and brick kilns.

Then, since the time I lived there, the city has been shaped by a violent, nationwide Maoist uprising, a brutal assassination of the royal family, a devastating earthquake and a Covid epidemic which swept through the city's tightly packed inhabitants. Sadly, the massive increase in population has brought with it an enormous increase in human suffering. While people leave the villages following the dream of better lives in the city, they often find themselves trapped in a prison of even greater suffering as they seek to survive the raw, harsh brutality which city life can bring.

And in the city, as well as across the nation, a whole group of people exist who mostly suffer in silence. They are the hidden sufferers, the ones who are afraid to speak out because their open cry for help will only invite more suffering by bringing shame upon the families, or communities, in which they live. These are women in nations like Nepal who have no voice and no one to help them. And this is where Anna comes in.

Anna is the real deal and her book will invite you into some of Nepal's hidden places where you will sit with women and hear their stories. They are stories of deep pain and suffering but they are also stories of wonderful redemption. They will touch your heart and at times you may find yourself reading through tear-filled eyes. Yet, you will read of hope and of one courageous woman who was determined to make a difference by setting up the amazing organization *Women Without Roofs*. This book had to be written and must be read.

The title of the book gives us an invitation to come with Anna to Kathmandu and as I read the manuscript I was definitely taken back to that amazing city. Anna has a wonderful insight into the people, especially women, of Nepal, and of how strongly the culture and religion plays a significant role in their lives. I was thrilled to read of places I had visited and of people I had known personally. I worshipped in some of the churches she mentions and shared rich fellowship with some of the people she talks about, including the incredible British missionary Eileen Lodge, who adopted local dress and customs and took on Nepali citizenship to serve the nation and people she loved. Her home was always open to us 'youngsters' whom she would supply with endless cups of *chai* (tea) and biscuits! The book took me back along the same dusty streets I had placed my feet and walked along in earlier days. I could experience the sounds and smells of the city and feel the crisp, clear air of the mountains as I read through its pages.

This is an amazing book and I pray that it will touch the hearts and lives of readers to do more for the women of Nepal, as well as the many other places where women suffer silently and alone. I'm thrilled to know that something is being done to help women like those mentioned within these pages. And I'm thankful that the message of Jesus, in places like Nepal, is changing the way people think and live their lives. Fears and superstitions are broken, people become valued regardless of class or caste and the position of women becomes elevated to equality with men.

Well done Anna on this amazing book. I pray that it will fall into the hands of people who will decide to make a difference and bring healing, help and justice to those who are suffering and oppressed. And I pray that the blessing of God will continue to be upon the wonderful organization *Women Without Roofs*.

Geoff Walvin, author of *Finding Faith in Unexpected Places*

Contents

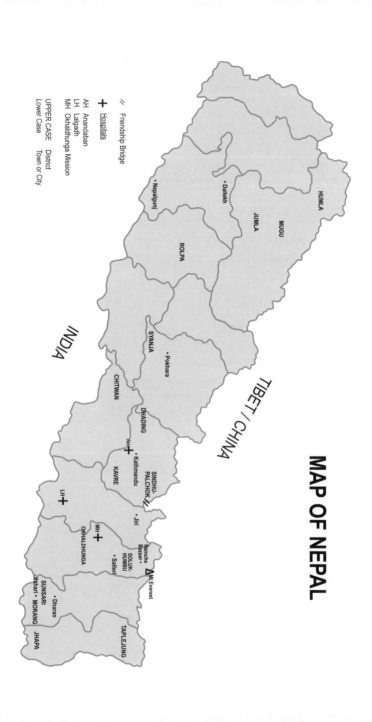

MAP OF NEPAL

TIBET / CHINA

INDIA

HUMLA

MUGU

JUMLA

• Dailekh

ROLPA

• Nepalgunj

SYANJA

• Pokhara

CHITWAN

DHADING

AH+ • Kathmandu

KAVRE

SINDHU-
PALCHOK //

• Jiri

LH+

MH+

OKHALDHUNGA

• Salleri

SOLU-
KHUMBU

Namche
Bazaar •

▲Mt.Everest

SUNSARI

Itahari •

• Dharan

MORANG

JHAPA

TAPLEJUNG

//   Friendship Bridge

+   Hospitals

AH   Anandaban
LH   Lalgadh
MH   Okhaldhunga Mission

UPPER CASE   District
Lower Case   Town or City

Introduction

I had forgotten how noisy the crows are in Kathmandu. They start cawing to each other early every morning and keep going all day until finally, they quieten down as darkness falls. Other than my husband, it seems they and the dogs barking in the distance are my only company during the enforced two-week coronavirus quarantine I am enduring having recently arrived in Nepal. It is early November 2020, and the global Covid-19 crisis is dragging on; in its wake are tragedy and ruin as people die, and businesses fail. Schools in Nepal are still closed because of the pandemic, so the usual early morning cacophony, as households prepare themselves for work and school by sweeping and washing pans, is muted. Only the animals seem to know it is the start of another day.

This is the second time that I have lived in Kathmandu. The last time I arrived was in 2004 when I turned up with my 6-month-old son, Zach, full of excitement and wonder to accompany my husband, Simon, at a two-year posting with the British Gurkhas. Soldiers from Nepal, known as Gurkhas, have served in the British Army for more than 200 years, and my husband is one in a long line of British officers to recruit and work with them.

I gave little thought then to the anxiety my son's grandparents must have felt as they waved us off in 2004; I simply longed for adventure and was delighted to have the chance to live in South Asia, a place I had been fascinated with since the age of 11. I was not disappointed; our time in Nepal changed the course of my life, and I came to know the most incredible and inspiring people.

Throughout my teenage years, I had corresponded with a pen pal in Calcutta, India and had read countless books about the region. Every book seemed to carry the same message, that India overwhelmed the senses and was a place that had to be experienced rather than read about. I resolved to follow this advice, and in 1997, while still at university, I had travelled to see my pen pal at her college in Delhi. As a result, I fell in love with the subcontinent. What struck me and intrigued me were the people; everywhere I looked, there was somebody doing something, and often those somethings were surprising. Perhaps there would be a man snoozing under a tree, traffic passing just inches from his face, maybe a family would be cooking food on a roundabout, or a peddler might be offering wet shaves to passers-by.

There was so much to take in, but I was also starting to notice that women remained hidden. Even when a homeless family lived in public view, the father might lounge about in the open, and the children might play at a close distance, but the mother of the family would be hidden away doing her chores, only appearing momentarily from inside their makeshift dwelling. I could not imagine the harshness and tedium of her life. Who else was hiding away from view?

Spending time in India was deeply challenging because of the entrenched poverty that I witnessed. I came home with a determination not to waste a penny and to give all the money I could spare to help the needy. I did not always achieve this, of course, but as a Christian, it also spurred me on to both pray for the poor and to learn about why there was so much poverty and injustice. I already knew that the Hindu caste system, which controls much of life in India and Nepal, was largely to blame, but I did not understand why the loving Christian God I knew and loved allowed such widespread suffering either. My search for an answer as to why God allows bad things to happen went even deeper when I experienced two miscarriages before my son was born.

It was during the early daze of parenthood when Zach was just ten days old and Simon was still at home on paternity leave that we had the phone call that changed everything. Simon was asked, simply and matter-of-factly, if he would like to go to Nepal or Brunei. Based on the fascination both of us had with South Asia, we chose Nepal, and the adventure began. I do not remember having any worries about taking a baby to a developing country; babies were born and grew up in Nepal all the time.

Within the first week of our arrival in 2004, we were confined to the house and under curfew. Twelve Nepali migrant workers in Iraq had been executed, and this provoked a wave of attacks against Arab and Muslim businesses in Kathmandu. We lived in the heart of Kathmandu, inside the bustling ring road, and violence broke out across the central part of the city. From our rooftop terrace, we could see tyres burning at key junctions less than a mile away on the ring road. Protests in Kathmandu almost always pass without injury or death, though there was significant property damage during the unrest.

At no point did I feel unsafe; it was the adventure I had been seeking, and we were fortunate to live in a large house, set back from the road, with guards on watch twenty-four hours a day.

Our guards did have a falling out, though, when the older of the two insisted the younger one came to our house to take over at the end of his shift. We had expressly told them not to switch because the curfew was in place. When the younger arrived, he was furious with us, even though we had not summoned him, and described how the police had tried to shoot at him as he made his way to our house. It turned out that the older guard was an alcoholic and, unable to have a drink with us about, had pretended that we had called the younger man to come in so he could sneak off and get a drink. Regrettably, we had to sack the older guard; it was only the end of our first week.

I'd like to be able to say that life calmed down somewhat after that, but I would be lying. There were frequent *bandhs* (strikes) when the Maoists called on shops and schools to close and all transportation to stop. On one occasion, we heard a bomb go off from the back of a taxi that was defying a strike, and once when on our way to the airport during another strike, rocks were thrown at our vehicle. I don't think I have told Zach's grandparents about this incident; it was a long time ago now, so I hope they will forgive me for involving their grandson in another escapade.

Both the bombing and the rock-throwing incidents were due to the actions of Nepal's Maoists. In 1996 a popular movement had begun among Nepal's rural and low caste population that sought to overthrow the patriarchal elites that were centred in Kathmandu. These elites had both ruled and owned much of Nepal's people and land for centuries. Inspired by China's Mao Zedong, these new Nepali Maoists took up arms to violently overthrow the oppressive social hierarchies they believed kept them in poverty. In many ways, their aims were not dissimilar to those of the peasant workers who rose up during the French Revolution centuries before.

When we arrived in Nepal during 2004, the Maoists controlled most of the hill country outside Nepal's major towns, and anyone wanting to travel or trek in these areas had to pay for a Maoist travel permit. Though they only cost about £10, they now fetch large amounts on eBay due to their rarity. The Maoists are no longer involved in an armed uprising, so these permits are not necessary anymore, thank goodness. Anyone who has watched the TV programme *Himalaya* with Michael Palin may recall that his British Gurkha guide, Adrian, is briefly kidnapped by the Maoists when the two of them go trekking. My husband is now doing Adrian's job in Kathmandu; let's hope there are no more kidnappings, however brief!

Back in Kathmandu and somewhat oblivious to the upheaval going on around us, we joined the international church where I was to meet Eileen Lodge. An elderly woman by then, she was still a force to be reckoned with and had been living in Nepal for almost fifty years. As a young missionary, she had been among the first outsiders to enter Nepal in the early 1950s. Eileen was a trained nurse and had helped to set up Shining Hospital near Pokhara, then Green Pastures Hospital, which is still going strong, and later on Lalgadh Hospital in Nepal's Terai (the lowland region of southern Nepal); her speciality was treating leprosy patients. Though she had given up her British citizenship to become a Nepali citizen, she still retained many British customs, including stopping each afternoon for tea served in cups and saucers by her loyal house staff, who had been with her for years.

It was over tea one afternoon while she and I were enjoying the heat of the winter sun, and Zach, who had just started walking, was playing with her house staff, that she asked for my help. The calm surroundings and pleasant atmosphere did not indicate the scale of what she was about to ask, nor the impact it would have on my life.

Throughout the years that Eileen had lived in Nepal, a small group of men and women had come to rely on her for their rent, medical bills and other basic needs. Eileen never sent anyone away empty-handed if they were in need. The arrangements were informal, and almost all of them were former leprosy patients, or their dependents, that Eileen had taken under her wing. She gave them money from her own limited funds, and they counted on her not only for financial assistance but to be their advocate. In Nepal's Hindu culture, the law of karma means that if something bad happens to you, such as leprosy, then it is because you deserve it. Even though someone may recover from leprosy, they are still stigmatized and ostracized by the wider society.

Quite simply, Eileen was concerned about what would happen to these people when she died. Already eighty years old and becoming more and more immobile, Eileen knew there needed to be a plan in place so that they were not abandoned in the future. As a great prayer warrior, she had been seeking God about what she should do and believed that God had told her someone from the British Camp would help. That someone was me.

Eileen's request was an answer to my prayers too. Faced with the hordes of poor people that I encountered each day in Kathmandu and already wrestling with God about why he allowed such suffering, I had increasingly come to understand that God was calling Christians to be his hands and feet on earth. On one particular day, the vehicle I was in got stuck in traffic at the busy Koteshwor intersection and I felt overwhelmed with the needs of the thousands of people also trying to get across the junction. I realised God was asking us to act and relieve the burden of poverty and injustice that these people, made in his image, bore. Without hesitation, I told

Eileen that I would help, and this was the beginning of Women Without Roofs (WWR).

Since I am an army wife, I had to leave Nepal at the end of my husband's two-year posting, and we returned to England, where I gave birth to my daughter. My heart belonged to Nepal, though, and I was always hoping and praying for an opportunity to return. I must confess that I had given up hope and assumed it would never happen. That was until a spreadsheet opened up on my husband's computer listing the job in Kathmandu that we had been hoping for. It came at the perfect time.

During the fifteen years since 2005, when I first said 'yes' to God and Eileen, WWR had grown steadily. There was no shortage of poverty-stricken people in Nepal, and those Eileen was already assisting told their needy friends that help was on offer, and they, in turn, told theirs. The message soon spread, and very quickly we appointed Esther, Eileen's trusted assistant, to help us run things on the ground. In the UK, a group of trustees got together, and the charity was formed and registered.

As the chair of trustees for WWR, I aimed to visit Nepal every couple of years to meet with Esther and the women we helped. This wasn't always easy with two young children, especially since Simon went on several tours to Afghanistan and wasn't around to look after them. His career also took us to America twice, which only increased the time and cost to get back to Nepal. Thankfully, God provided fantastic trustees for me to work with, and they were able to visit Nepal more frequently than I did.

When I did get back to Nepal for short visits, I would spend hectic days racing around Kathmandu, visiting the women we helped. WWR had purchased a moped for Esther, so the two of us would swaddle our faces to keep the dirt out and take to Kathmandu's dusty roads. As we crisscrossed the city, trying to meet with everyone, the thrill of being back in the city I loved would sometimes overwhelm me.

These visits were also full of heartache. All the women WWR supports are on their own for one reason or another. Many are widows, though not all of them are elderly, and there is a large group of women in their thirties who have been abandoned by their husbands. It appears that the pressure of providing for a young family is too much for some Nepali men, and they simply walk out, never to be heard of again. The ladies had tragic stories, and though it was my privilege to sit in their dark rooms listening to their secret stories of loss and pain, I felt powerless to truly change the circumstances they found themselves in. The Hindu concept of karma, that one gets what one deserves, means that if a woman loses her husband to cancer, for instance, she is blamed and regarded as bad luck. This causes further ostracization from her family and community, just when she needs it the most.

Thankfully, we have a good God, and he continued to bless WWR so that our influence grew; we have always had just enough to provide for the needs we encounter in Nepal. We invited a group of church pastors in Kathmandu to be on the lookout for women that needed our help, and soon after, they formed a committee so that WWR could be formally registered as a non-governmental organization (NGO). In 2011 we opened our first women's home, Anugraha Ashram (Grace Women's Home) to house the most vulnerable women WWR supports. When we had to close it in 2017, we relocated to Mahima Griha (Glory House) in the heart of Kathmandu.

Politically, Nepal has seen tremendous change throughout the intervening years since I last lived here. Just after we left in 2006, there was a ceasefire with the Maoists, and in the political scrum that followed, the Maoists were elected by popular and democratic vote to Nepal's government. Yet, following several years of inaction and internal squabbles, they were promptly voted out. Officially no longer a Hindu monarchy, Nepal is now a secular republic; Christmas can be celebrated, and in theory, Christians and churches are no longer prohibited. In reality, though, neither are all that welcome and as a Christian NGO, WWR has also encountered some of this persecution. Hurdles are put in our way by the local government at every opportunity.

The country has also had to handle more than its fair share of natural disasters. A devastating earthquake killed several thousand in 2015, destroying whole villages and countless buildings in towns and cities across the country. The annual monsoon rains also cause countless landslides and flooding that can sweep away homes, families and even villages.

This brings me to 2020, and now the whole world is battling with the Covid-19 pandemic. I am overwhelmed and delighted to be back living in Kathmandu, but also filled with a desperate longing to be useful. Sadly, Eileen died last year, and I already miss her presence as a prayer warrior. In my enforced quarantine, I feel as if I am an animal in a cage, impatient to get out and experience the vibrant city around me, whose sounds I can faintly hear.

I am extremely curious to know more about what God is doing among women in Nepal. I know he is at work since the Nepali church is one of the fastest-growing in the world. Simon and I have begun watching the English language services that the local Nepali church is broadcasting during the lockdown. Sadly, though, there are no women involved in these services, and so I have started to wonder why they are hidden. Where are they, and what stories do they have to tell?

From my conversations with the women that WWR helps in their tucked-away rooms, I know their faith is strong, and they have a desire for their stories to be told. Some have written to me over the years with warnings for other women, anxious that the injustices they have faced are not repeated with the next generation. In Nepal, anything written is given a value of truth, so by recording their stories, I aim to encourage them and bear witness to their struggles and successes.

I hope you'll come with me to Kathmandu to meet them.

In my narrative, all the women and our staff's names have been changed to protect them. I have chosen aliases for them that are traditional Nepali names. The women's family members are referred to without using names as her brother, sister, father, cousin etc. I hope this doesn't become too irritating for the reader, and in each instance, it is clear to whom I am referring.

During the year I spent interviewing the women, I took plenty of videos and photos. These can be found on YouTube and Instagram under the profile 'DislocatedChristians'.

A short history of Nepal

Due to its extreme topography, the united country of Nepal did not exist until almost two hundred and fifty years ago. Instead, the land now known as Nepal consisted of distinct tribal groups that occupied and ruled their own valleys. For the most part, the hills and mountains kept these tribal hill states separate from each other. Still, some notable warlords tried to extend their territories, which led to violent skirmishes between the small kingdoms. In the late eighteenth century, Prithvi Narayan Shah, the ruler of the modest but central principality of Gorkha, led his troops on a victorious campaign and merged the independent hill states into one country, now known as Nepal.

According to legend, Prithvi Narayan Shah was cursed as a young man. He encountered a holy man in a forest to whom he offered a milky curd drink. The holy man drank the curd and then regurgitated it back into the cup before asking Prithvi Narayan Shah to drink it. Upon Prithvi's refusal, the holy man cursed the Shah dynasty. He prophesied that the family would rule Nepal for only ten generations and afterwards would be obliterated.

At the start of the nineteenth century, the British East India Company pushed northwards from India and attempted to invade Nepal. Nepal's combatants, led by Gorkha chiefs, successfully held them off, and neither side could claim victory. Impressed by the bravery of the Nepali soldiers, the East India Company signed a peace treaty with Nepal in 1816 and asked permission to recruit Gurkha fighters into their army. This established the Gurkha regiments that have served in the British and Indian armies ever since.

In the mid nineteenth century, following a bloody massacre in Kathmandu, Jung Bahadur Rana became prime minister. He relegated the Shah royal family to mere figureheads. For more than a hundred years, the Rana family maintained an unusual hereditary government whereby all prime ministers and senior bureaucrats had to descend from the Rana line. They kept the royal family under house arrest for a century.

A democracy movement, supported by the Shah King, overthrew the Ranas in the 1950s, but by 1960, King Mahendra decided he wasn't keen on democracy and took absolute control. In the space of ten years, Nepal had switched from one autocratic regime, the Ranas, to another, the royals. As a result, this eventually led to the People's Movement in 1990, which saw Nepal's population unite to call for democracy. In turn, this inspired the Maoist armed insurgency that resulted in so much bloodshed during the 1990s and 2000s.

Another massacre occurred in June 2001 when the crown prince, angered by the queen's refusal to allow him to choose a bride, turned a gun on the royal family before killing himself. Nine royal family members died during the mass shooting, and Nepal's population, already in turmoil due to the Maoist uprising, despaired with their rulers. The former king's brother became the new king, and in 2005 he ousted the corrupt government and took absolute control of the nation. This was the final straw for Nepal's people and only served to increase their support for the Maoists.

In 2006 the Maoists' demand that Nepal become a democratic secular republic was met, and the king agreed to step down, thus ending the rule of the Shahs. The holy man's curse had come true; the Shahs had reigned Nepal for exactly ten generations, and as foretold, most had been obliterated during the 2001 massacre. Had the prophecy really been uttered all those generations before, or was it a skilful piece of propaganda that helped the Maoists secure the fall of the Shahs? Nepal's people, for the most part, believe in the power of the curse.

As for the history of religion in Nepal, geography has also played a role in shaping the people's beliefs. For centuries, Nepal's tribes practised animism and worshipped the mountains, animals and plants they saw around them. Being so cut off from the rest of the world, they developed strong superstitions based on the actions of the weather and disease.

In the south of Nepal, the small town of Lumbini found fame as the birthplace of Buddha. His teachings incorporated many of the ancient animist traditions. Buddhism spread from Nepal north into Tibet, and in turn, Tibetan people groups migrating south brought back a more formalized and established form of Buddhism with them. As a consequence, many monasteries, *stupas* (dome-shaped buildings) and prayer wheels can be seen across Nepal. Buddhist prayer flags appear all over the country, in both bustling towns and adorning remote mountainsides.

For more than two thousand years, Indian migrants have brought Hinduism with them north into Nepal. Since Hinduism recognizes many gods, it coexists with Buddhism reasonably easily, and Buddha is recognized by Hindus as a deity. Almost all temple complexes in Nepal have both Hindu and Buddhist elements, and it isn't easy to separate the two religions. The Hindu caste system has been superimposed on Nepali society, but adherence to it isn't nearly as vehement as in India.

One area where there is a growing disparity between the two religions is the attitude to animal sacrifice. At major festivals, thousands of animals are sacrificed to pacify the Hindu gods but devoted Buddhists, who may take vows of non-violence and attempt to avoid even stepping on insects, disapprove. In recent years, protests against the gratuitous slaughter of animals have taken place at significant temple sites.

Nowadays, religion is more often a personal practice, and there is less corporate and community adherence except at major festivals. Gurus espouse their teachings on YouTube and invite their followers to spend time on retreat at ashrams. As with religion in the West, the commercialization of religion and the ability of the internet and smartphones to bring teachings directly to people are forming a new type of religious follower.

Nepal is now secular, but many would like the royal family to be reinstated; in particular, Nepal's Hindus who believe the royal family are incarnations of Hindu gods. Muslims and

Christians also live within the country's borders, and sadly there are regular reports of religiously motivated attacks against them.

Given the country's turbulent history, its propensity to earthquakes, distance from ports (making global trade difficult) and the mountainous terrain, achieving economic development is extremely difficult. It is likely that a stable and prosperous Nepal will remain elusive, hence Nepal's status as the 142nd developed country in the world. Politics and religion are intertwined, and daily life is affected by both. The nation's future will depend on whether the country can remain a secular democracy and ensure religious freedom for all its people.

1

Evangelist: Lila

At last, the day of my freedom arrived – the end of quarantine. I had got so used to spending my time in the house, and walking laps of our garden, that as I stepped out into the bustling streets of Kathmandu, I had to fight against a sense of agoraphobia.

My priority now that I could leave the house was to meet up with Esther, and as we walked to a courtyard restaurant to spend time catching up, I almost missed noticing that the mountains were visible. Kathmandu's streets were nothing like the clean and well-constructed pavements that I was used to in Britain. The paving slabs were laid higgledy-piggledy, and there was a lot of dog mess and litter to avoid. I was concentrating so hard on where I was walking that my eyes were focused down rather than up, to where the mountains had majestically appeared. I was also recalling fond memories of pushing Zach's pushchair along these pavements; going just a few hundred yards was enough to provide a full-body workout.

Kathmandu is one of the most polluted cities in the world; its bowl-shaped valley traps the woodsmoke and exhaust fumes produced by the valley's nearly three million inhabitants, and in a typical year, the breathtaking Himalayas are visible for only one or two weeks. One of the upsides to Covid has been a reduction in traffic and pollution, and there are now many more opportunities to view the snow-topped peaks. I was overjoyed that today, on my first day of freedom, they were sparkling in the sun.

Esther and I were delighted to be back in each other's company again and could not stop talking and smiling. As we caught up, our conversation ranged across all manner of topics; we discussed everything from plumbing to weddings. WWR was about to install a new water pump at the women's home, and the landlord was not maintaining things as he should be. In contrast, one of our staff members, Somi, was about to get married, and due to the complicated situation she found herself in, the marriage would benefit her son rather than her. (See Chapter 3.) Esther patiently explained all these situations to me, and I asked her endless questions.

Frustratingly, walking anywhere in Kathmandu leaves me with a sore throat due to the heavy pollution. A traditional and widely available remedy for this is drinking hot water with lemon, ginger and honey, which has an instant soothing effect. It was while we were both sipping this pleasant mixture that I introduced the idea of this book and explained that I wanted to tell the stories of Nepal's Christian women, who have so often been overlooked and whose stories remain untold. Esther was enthralled by the idea, and we drew up plans to visit women who we knew had incredible stories to tell. At the top of our list was Lila. She is one of the original women that Eileen had asked me to support, and having been healed from leprosy, she was now a Christian evangelist. She had once written to me in England with her story, and I was confident that she would like others to hear about her life. We made plans to visit her as soon as possible.

A few Sundays later, we drove around the side of the airport to Thapagaon, where Lila's home is situated. On the way, I spotted the Buddha Air hangar. I have always thought Buddha Air was a particularly amusing name for an airline; in my mind, it conjures up images of pilots and passengers levitating their way to far-flung destinations. I was quickly brought back to reality, though, by the crazy overtaking occurring on Kathmandu's ring road; cars crossed into oncoming traffic to overtake, and even crazier drivers would pull across to the far side of the road to overtake the overtakers, at even higher speeds. I found myself holding my breath as they performed their insane acts.

Lila's home is tucked away from the main road and accessed through a maze of paths. Once we had found the gate to her home, we received a warm welcome from her, and we settled down on her bed, which doubled up as a sofa, to listen to her. Lila sat proudly on her other bed-cum-sofa. It was obvious to me that some of her fingers were missing due to leprosy, but whenever I have met her, she has never been ashamed of this. In a country such as Nepal, where disfigurement is assumed to indicate bad karma, she confidently displays her gnarled hands as a testimony to her life and healing.

If she had been born in England, I could easily imagine Lila living in the wealthy Home Counties as the matriarch of a large and successful family. Now almost 70 years old, she is still bright and well-informed; it is clear that her opinions hold weight, and there's a little bit of Hyacinth Bucket[1] about her. When we visited, she was dressed in a bright pink *kurta* (also known as a salwar kameez, it consists of a long top, matching trousers and scarf) covered in roses. Though her hair was dyed black and neatly tied back, there was a wide streak of grey at her roots. Unfortunately, life has been extremely hard on her, and she did not have the opportunity to raise a family, so she lives alone.

Starting with the circumstances of her birth, Lila began her story.

Lila was the fourth and last child born to her parents. An older brother had died when he was just ten days old, and then more tragedy ensued. Her father died when her mother was eight months pregnant with Lila. This catastrophic event took place when her mother was just 20 years old, and so she was left as an extremely young widow with three children to raise. To ease the pressure on her mother, Lila's older sister was sent to live with her grandparents, but since girls were not valued in Nepali culture, she was neglected by them and became so malnourished that she resorted to eating mud. This sister died at the age of 7, and so by the time Lila was 4, half of her immediate family were dead.

Lila's family home was in Kavre, the district that borders Kathmandu on the eastern side of the valley, yet her family also owned some land in the Kathmandu Valley which was, inexplicably, considered worthless at the time. This land is where Lila's home is located today, and it is valued at millions of rupees now. With so little flat land that can be easily built upon, land prices have soared in Kathmandu Valley to the extent that some pockets of land cost more than the equivalent in New York or Mumbai.

The caste system has a huge influence on life in Nepal, and everyone knows where they stand within its structure. In its simplest form, the four caste levels are based on parts of the body. At the top are the Brahmins that take their status from being associated with the head of Lord Brahma's body, hence the name 'Brahmin'; they are the intellectuals and priests and considered most clean. Next come the warrior castes that take their role from the arms and torso. Below them are the traders that fulfil the needs of the stomach, and beneath them are the unclean castes associated with the legs; they are tailors, cobblers and carry out all manner of menial tasks. Below all of these are the untouchable castes, or Dalits, that are not even considered part of the body. They are treated as polluted and as inferior to everyone else, though their status is improving as human rights, and awareness of their plight, have been promoted worldwide.

Lila hails from a high caste Brahmin family, and consequently, purity is highly valued. For that reason, according to the custom of her family, girls had to be married before their first period. Lila had an arranged marriage at the age of 10 and found herself living away from her mother with her 14-year-old husband and his parents near Kathmandu. His home was adjacent to the plot of land on which she lives today.

Lila described her mother-in-law as kind, which certainly benefited her because she managed to spend a week or two at the newly opened Gandhi School. This was Lila's only participation in formal education, and she remained illiterate until teaching herself to read many years after. Later, her in-laws also gave her time to seek treatment for her illness. According to Lila, she wasn't all that busy at her in-laws' house; there was no farming, she only needed to tend the cows and goats and help out with rice planting once a year during the annual festival.

It is common to hear stories of horrific abuse against daughters-in-law by their mothers-in-law. Sometimes, girls are forced into early marriages to simply help out with housework in their husband's home, where tradition dictates they must live. Mothers-in-law can be cruel taskmasters if they consider the performance of these girls to be unsatisfactory. Often, the only way to improve the situation for these young wives is for them to bear a son themselves so that they can marry them off early to bring a new girl into the home. Sadly, the cycle begins again as the once-abused mother-in-law takes out her vengeance on her new daughter-in-law. Worse still are the consequences for a girl who is unable to bear a son.

Lila's aunt had helped to arrange her marriage and lived nearby. This aunt was friendly to Lila and was someone that she could confide in. When Lila's first period arrived, she was able to ask her aunt what was happening, and this triggered another ritual to mark the occasion. Brahmin tradition specifies that when their periods begin, girls must be hidden from the male members of their family for fifteen days, and the girl's father should present his daughter with new clothes and jewellery. Since Lila's father had died, her older brother graciously fulfilled this role for her.

During her subsequent periods, Lila had to confine herself to a cattle shed and stay away from other members of her family. This practice is known as *chhaupadi* and requires girls to remain in small huts for the duration of their period each month and in the immediate days after giving birth. Confinement is believed necessary because the girls are regarded as impure while menstruating or bleeding, though, in fact, the risk of confinement is far greater than any imagined threat the girls pose to men. Throughout the years, thousands of girls have become severely infected while living in dirty spaces and have also died from pneumonia and smoke inhalation due to desperate attempts to keep warm in outhouses. In 2005, *chhaupadi* was banned by Nepal's supreme court, but regrettably, it is still practised in rural areas today. During Lila's teenage years in the 1960s, it was a common practice, especially among Brahmin families.

When Lila was just 14 years old, she noticed that something was wrong with her body. Her feet had become dreadfully cracked, and her breasts were not developing (I have been unable to confirm whether this symptom is a true sign of leprosy;

it may have indicated more general malnutrition and poor health). Her family's first response to this was to invite a *jhakri*, a witchdoctor or shaman, to heal her. The *jhakri* performed a fire ritual by waving a flaming torch over her face and head. The shaman then invited the snake god, whom her family revered, to cure her. Though she had not received a proper diagnosis, her family and neighbours began to gossip that her affliction may be leprosy.

Even though something was evidently wrong with Lila, her in-laws did nothing to help her in a practical sense. According to the rules of her caste, wearing shoes in the home was prohibited, and she must not wear them when collecting water either. Her brother, upon finding out that her feet were painfully cracked, provided shoes for her, but her in-laws hid them from her, such was their insistence on maintaining purity and caste law.

Despite their high status and supposed superiority to others, many practices particularly disadvantage high caste women from doing well in life. Strict adherence to laws of purity among them means that girls are trained to be especially subservient and naïve. Whereas women from other castes may be permitted to have more of a flexible approach to life, which leads to an ability to turn their hand to whatever needs doing, a Brahmin girl is raised to remain hidden and to submit herself to the decisions made for her by men. If tragedy befalls a high-caste woman, and a man is not able to represent her or make choices for her, unfortunately she is often ill-prepared to take on that role for herself.

Thankfully, Lila's spirit had not yet been completely crushed by the strictures of her caste, and at the age of 14, she was still able to think and act for herself. When the fire rituals made no difference to her health, she decided to take herself to a hospital.

She headed to Bir Hospital, in the centre of Kathmandu, which is still functioning today. Though her feet were the cause of her troubles, she walked to the hospital, around five miles, and back again. At the hospital, she remembers paying 25 paise (less than a quarter of one penny) for an X-ray, and her blood was taken for testing. A swab test for tuberculosis (TB), a common ailment in Nepal at the time, was also performed.

In the following four days, Lila walked to the hospital and back home again, turning up each day to find out if the test results were available and what the diagnosis was. On each of these days, she crossed the busy Koteshwor junction, where roads from the three cities (Kathmandu, Patan and Bhaktapur) in the Kathmandu Valley intersect. Heading home after meeting with Lila this very evening, I was to queue at this junction for forty-five minutes; it is hellishly busy. It is also the crossroads where God spoke to me in 2004 about setting up WWR and acting to help the hordes of people I saw around me in need. It seems God has been using this junction, and the people who go through it, to work out his purposes for quite some time now.

As Lila went across the Koteshwor junction twice a day for four days, she was spotted. A woman with leprosy, who was placed outside her home so that she was kept occupied by watching the crowds go by, saw Lila going to and fro. This woman, whose name Lila does not recall, asked her why she was walking by with such purpose and regularity. Lila explained that she was visiting the hospital and described her symptoms. Without explaining her reasons, the woman invited Lila to come back on Thursday and not to wear her gold. As a member of a high caste, Lila would have proudly worn much of her dowry daily; she would be less conspicuous without it.

When Lila returned on Thursday, the two of them walked together to Shanta Bhawan Hospital in Sanepa, which was run by missionaries. Shanta Bhawan means Palace of Peace, and the building was a former Rana palace; it was known for its calm atmosphere and foreign doctors. On Thursdays, there was a clinic, run by doctors from Anandaban Leprosy Hospital, that Lila's helpful new friend knew about.

God was already mindful of Lila and provided help when she needed it. On arrival at the hospital, Lila was asked to provide various pieces of information so that she could be registered. This included her father's name, that of her husband, and her age. Shockingly, she did not know any of this. In Nepal, it is considered bad luck to say someone's name out loud, as it is believed that this identifies them to evil spirits, and so family members are referred to as 'husband', 'father', 'big sister', 'littlest sister' etc. Birthdates and birthdays are also unimportant. Miraculously, a man was present at the hospital who claimed to know Lila, her father (who had died fourteen years previously) and her husband, so he provided the missing information. Lila lied about her age and alleged that she was 18 years old. Once she was through the registration process, all the treatment at Shanta Bhawan was free, which was fantastic news given that it was obvious to everyone there that Lila had the first signs of leprosy.

As Lila told her story, I was quickly becoming a fan of her brother. After all, he dutifully fulfilled the caste rituals when her period began and then provided shoes for her. When Lila was advised to become an inpatient at Anandaban Leprosy Hospital, he did not shun her as her husband did and instead accompanied her on the fifteen-mile walk into the jungle to where the hospital is located. He helped carry her belongings and ensured she reached the hospital safely. I have stayed at this hospital for a church weekend, and it spooked me even then; friends were kept awake all night hunting for a huge and elusive spider they had spotted under their bed.

Lila and her brother set off at 5 a.m. and arrived in time for the main meal of the day at 11 a.m. Until this point, Lila told me, she was not scared of having leprosy, not even when the shaman performed the fire ritual. However, when she arrived at the hospital and saw the other deformed leprosy patients for the first time, she felt fear.

Lila remained at Anandaban hospital for one month and fully participated in life there. Though trained medical staff performed all the clinical work, it was left to the patients to run the hospital and to do all the cooking, cleaning and maintenance. Lila was struck by the willingness of everyone to accept each other, and within just a few days, she no longer felt fearful. On Thursday evenings, there was a Bible fellowship, run by the wives of the doctors, that everyone attended; the message was that each of them should be friendly to each other. Again, this was a new idea to Lila, who had thus far been taught to remain pure by avoiding others who could supposedly contaminate her by their low status or afflictions.

At the end of the month, Lila returned to live at her mother's home, where her brother and sister-in-law also lived. Now that her leprosy diagnosis had been confirmed, her husband and in-laws rejected her, and she was no longer welcome in their home. She received a prescription for medicine to combat leprosy, and she continued to take this for the next ten years until her disease was finally and fully cured.

Lila was still only 14 years old and had already been married, abandoned by her husband, and dealt with leprosy. As I sat listening to this remarkable story, I could not help but think of my 14-year-old daughter, Beth. To my mind, Beth has her whole life ahead of her, and the possibilities are endless. For Lila, at the same age, her future was already closed off and severely limited. It would be very unlikely that anyone would marry her again, so there would be no opportunity for her to have a family, and she would need to live with the consequences of leprosy for her whole life. I felt dreadfully sad for the teenage Lila. Yet, God had not forgotten her.

At the age of 17, Lila returned to Anandaban since she was still having some pain and her prescription needed to be adjusted. This time she remained at the hospital for six weeks, and God met with her powerfully. Once again, she enjoyed the congenial atmosphere and took part in the Bible fellowships. Though Lila had never fully embraced Hindu beliefs and had simply participated in the rituals because everybody she knew did so, she began to see the difference between Christian living and her way of life until now. Lila had witnessed the ostracism that her mother had experienced when her husband (Lila's father) had passed away. Once again, the laws of karma labelled her mother as unfortunate and ill-fated. The devout Hindu community they were part of had eschewed the family, but as Lila spent more time with Christians, she saw that they cared for one another and shunned no one.

Lila shared a room with a Christian lady called Padma. One night, Lila had a dream in which Jesus appeared to her; as she describes this to me, Lila's face is beaming. In the dream, Jesus said the strange words 'John 15:5' to her. She had no idea what this odd code meant, so when she woke up, she asked her roommate if she knew. Padma told her it was a Bible verse, and together, they looked up the reference. When Lila read the words 'remain in me' from the Bible, she knew that she had to give her life to Christ and become a Christian.

Upon returning home to her mother and sister-in-law, Lila was a changed woman and actively avoided the Hindu rites and rituals that had been part of her life until now. She also brought a Bible back from Anandaban with her and was determined to learn how to read it. As she pored over it each evening, her mother would berate her for wasting kerosene.

At *Dashain* (Nepal's largest festival), matters came to a head. During this festival, family members are required to bless each other by placing *tikas*, red dots made of vermillion powder, on each other's foreheads. A *tika* symbolizes the third eye associated with many Hindu gods so Christians avoid receiving these blessings. Lila refused to honour her brother by placing a *tika* on him and would not accept this Hindu blessing from the other members of her family. In a rage, her mother instructed her to kill herself.

Lila was not deterred and was baptized shortly afterwards. Her new church family, which met in secret, went to the Suryabinayak jungle near Bhaktapur, where they dug out a modest pond at the bottom of a waterfall. She, along with six others, was baptized there, and the small group of believers ate a picnic to celebrate afterwards. At this time, the young Nepali church was growing rapidly, and the following weekend there was another baptism service. Lila wished to attend this service, but her mother beat her, so she was unable to go.

This was the beginning of a prolonged period of persecution at the hands of her family. Lila's mother and sister-in-law would not allow her into the family's kitchen since Christians were considered unclean. Lila regularly went without food. On one occasion, she did not eat for a whole week. By this time, Lila had a young nephew, and he saved the day by telling his father, Lila's heroic brother, that she was being denied food. Her brother was unaware of what was happening because he travelled a lot for work. Upon finding out from his son that she was slowly being starved, he put his foot down and ordered his wife and mother to feed her.

When her brother was away, the ostracism from her family continued, and Lila could only put up with being oppressed like this for so long. Eventually, it took its toll. Given that her chance to have a family of her own had most likely been lost at such a young age, she felt that she had nothing to live for, and so she decided to kill herself.

Traditional houses in Kathmandu are three storeys tall, and each floor has a name. When Zach was a toddler, he had a book that contained a rhyme to help him remember these: *chhidi*, *matan* and *buigal*. As Lila spoke in Nepali about the *buigal*, and as I tried my best to understand her, I was able to see that it was a significant place for her. Whenever she mentioned it, a shadow came over her face, and she looked down in shame. I felt apprehensive about the translation that Esther was about to provide for me.

It was in the *buigal* that Lila hung a rope over a beam and looped the rope around her neck. Her mother and neighbours were sat outside but began to wonder why the house was so quiet and asked where Lila had got to. Her mother came into the house and up to the *buigal*. She entered the room right before Lila was going to pull on the rope. It was a close call, but thankfully, Lila was prevented from taking her own life and from this moment on, her mother was not so cruel to her.

I asked Lila how she became known as an evangelist, and she continued with her story. Having achieved a far better understanding with her mother, Lila began praying and fasting about what God's plan might be for her life. As she worked in the paddies with other farming families, she sang Christian songs and could not be quiet about her faith. Her pastor at the nascent Gyaneshwar Church (Kathmandu's second oldest church) recognized her conviction and invited her to help at the church. With the pastor's wife, she returned to Shanta Bhawan Hospital to visit patients and to pray for them. Lila was also asked to attend a sewing and weaving course and, after two years, became the instructor on the course.

Eventually, Lila was encouraged to attend a Bible college for two years; she was 27 years old at the time and attended along with three other women and ten men. Her tuition fees were paid for by a pastor from Kerala, in southern India, who had recently been deported from Nepal under threat of imprisonment if he did not leave. Lila proudly told me that she finished top of her class; the others all had to drop out for one reason or another!

It seems that Nepal's government was aware that the Bible college existed and monitored it but did not, at that time, arrest the lecturers or students. I suspect that since the number of Christians in Kathmandu was so small then, they were not perceived as a threat. This changed in the 1980s, and persecution of Christians intensified; the police even undertook covert operations. On one occasion, a squad of undercover police attended a church service at Putalisadak, Kathmandu's oldest church. *Putali* means butterfly and *sadak* means road; it's a beautiful name for a church, and speaks to me of freedom and new life. At the end of the service, they seized the pastor along with the church records. Lila's name was on the church register, so she was now a wanted woman.

One evening, just after she had finished teaching at a youth fellowship, the police turned up to detain her. She escaped them by only minutes as she fled out a back door. The following week, the police turned up at Gandhi Ashram, where she taught the sewing and weaving class, and having missed her there too, they finally came to her home. As Lila explained this to me, her hands were gesticulating wildly as she described the cat and mouse games that they played with her. She was overjoyed that in each instance, the police missed her by just minutes, and she credited God for helping her evade them by guiding her down roads and alleys.

God continued to protect Lila while scores of Christians across the city were being arrested and held in prison. On one occasion, she fearlessly went to a jail to visit two pastors. While speaking with them, she overheard the prison officers talking about her, wondering if she could be a Christian too and if they should arrest her. Before they could do anything, she escaped the building and ran off.

A brief reprieve for Nepal's Christians came in 1990 when the country inched towards democracy following a people's movement. Throughout the 1980s, Lila had been praying for freedom of religion so that the oppression of Christians would cease. On 7 April 1990, she was stopped on the street by a television crew and asked what she wanted for Nepal. In what I cannot help thinking was a prophetic declaration, she told them she wished for freedom of religion. Her words were broadcast live to the nation, and later that evening, fellow Christians told her she had been foolish to make such a bold claim on a public platform. She stood by her words, and the following day, to the surprise of the nation, the king removed the constitutional ban on political parties and ushered in a period of relative religious freedom.

I asked her what it is like to live in Nepal as a Christian today. She said it is very difficult; they cannot preach or produce leaflets about their faith. Some church leaders are still in prison. She told me about a pastor in Pokhara (one of Nepal's major cities) who had been recently arrested. He had appeared in a YouTube video in which he asked his congregation to pray against coronavirus. Rather than ending up in prison, he had paid a hefty fine and been released.

I suggested that if Christians entered politics in Nepal, they might be able to bring about more freedom for churches; sadly, she felt that all politicians, no matter if they were Christian or not, ended up being corrupted by money and power. In the days before and after my visit to her, there had been protests in Kathmandu calling for the reinstatement of the monarchy, which was dismissed in 2006 when Nepal became a secular republic. She backed these protests and felt a benign dictator, such as their king had been, was better than the corrupt multi-party democracy the country had been putting up with since 2006. This surprised me as Nepal was a Hindu kingdom when the king was in power, and he was revered as the incarnation of the Hindu god Vishnu. How would this benefit Nepal's Christians?

Lila was also saddened by the proliferation of different Christian denominations and the infighting between them. She prayed regularly for unity among the churches, especially during lockdown when she used the extra time for worship and supplication.

On a personal level, she felt that she had a lot to be grateful for. Her mother had died in 1999, shortly after becoming a Christian, and her brother, my hero, had given her the land that her house was built upon. She is one of the few ladies that WWR supports who only receives money to pay her medical bills; almost everyone else receives funds for rent as well. Sadly, neither her brother nor sister-in-law came to know Jesus before passing away, which disappointed her. In the 1990s, the leprosy mission had paid for the bricks and concrete that she had built her house with. Two nieces and two nephews remained alive, and she was delighted that her nieces had both married Christians. She hopes to bequeath her land to her nieces, but one nephew is contesting this.

Before I departed from Lila, I asked her to look up Philippians 1:3–6. Since I do not speak Nepali especially well, I have found that gifting a Bible verse to the women we work with is a good way to let them know how I'm praying for them. Lila had developed a unique way of turning the wafer-thin pages of her Bible with her contorted hands. She would turn over clumps of pages as best she could and then use her breath to blow the pages apart. It was a little slow but worked perfectly, and her method was beautiful for its uniqueness.

It was cold and dark as Esther and I left Lila, and we flipped on torches to help us navigate the narrow paths from her house back to the main road. Leaving Lila that evening was akin to exiting a cathedral, there was so much majesty in her story, and I was awed by what God had done in her life; the world outside seemed trifling in comparison. As we queued through Koteshwor *chowk*, the centre of Koteshwor, where she had also traipsed on her search for a diagnosis and where God had begun to reveal himself to her, I felt overawed again. In all the noise and crowds, he had been mindful of Lila and had drawn her to himself. Not only had she received physical healing but emotional and spiritual too. God had provided a new family for her through his church, and I know he has not stopped using her life for his glory.

2

Seeker: Tanya

'Do you know where SalesBerry's is?' Well, yes, I thought I did as I had been there once before, and if I was wrong, then Google would direct me to where it was. Esther told me she would meet me at the first gate into SalesBerry's and lead me from there to the WWR's women's home where Tanya lives, and so I set off early one Thursday morning to find her and SalesBerry department store. The Covid pandemic was still raging, and we were banned from using taxis; since I did not yet have a driving licence for Nepal, I had to walk.

The first part of the journey was straightforward but unpleasant as the route took me alongside the ring road for nearly a mile. It is eight lanes wide in this part of the capital and full of vehicles that pump out noxious exhaust fumes. It is incredibly noisy too. However, there are plenty of sights and curious buildings to discover, if you look carefully; for instance, the ambitiously named Einstein Academy and its 'libary' [sic]. The ring road was widened just a few years ago when buildings on either side of the road were bulldozed. The houses and shops that now face onto the highway were formerly down obscure side streets, and they still do not seem prepared for the onslaught of traffic that passes them all day and night.

There are new pedestrian footbridges over the wide ring road, and these afford a brief glimpse of the mountains if it is one of Kathmandu's clear days. Oddly, these footbridges are never finished off properly, and on arriving at the bottom of their steps, a jump down is often required onto an unfinished verge or into a roadside ditch. Getting to a pavement often involves climbing over or through a fence. The result of these obstacles is that only the cowardly, like me, use the footbridges and hordes of brave (or perhaps foolish) Nepalis still take their chances crossing the ring road despite the heavy traffic.

Having survived the madness of the ring road, I tried to locate SalesBerry. It turns out that I did not know where it was, and since I did not yet have a sim card to allow me to use data while out and about, I could not rely on Google to rescue me. Eventually, I figured out that I had taken the wrong street off the ring road and made my way to where Esther was expecting me. She appeared out of the crowds and waved me over to her.

During our walk to the women's home, Esther pointed out land on the far side of the road that her brother owned. He was renting it out to a small hospital, and adjacent to it was more property that her family had sold. I learn so much going anywhere with Esther in Kathmandu, as her family has lived here for generations; she has connections to so many people and places, and it is fascinating to hear her tell the history of the places we visit. Today, though, she was feeling upset with Nepali politicians who concentrate all government jobs and departments in Kathmandu. In turn, this has led to centralization and a massive demand for land in the capital, pushing property prices beyond the reach of the locals. Nepal's only international airport is in Kathmandu, and both of us hope that when new international airports are opened in Pokhara

and Lumbini, Nepal will become less centralized, and more of
the country will have a chance to flourish.

The next part of our walk to the small women's home that
WWR runs took us alongside one of the major routes out of
Kathmandu to Godavari. Though the road is not as wide as the
ring road, it makes a steep descent, hence the busy traffic on
the other side has to rev their engines to get up the hill, making
more noise and pouring out more fumes. After turning off this
road at the bottom of the hill, we finally made our way through
a maze of back lanes, of which not even one is straight, to find
the home. By the time I arrived, I had a headache from the noise
and fumes and was relieved to take off my Covid face mask.

Despite my grumpiness, when I reached the home, the ladies offered me a wonderful welcome, and I soon relaxed as
their hospitality and warmth won me over. WWR has run a
small women's home for nine years (it has switched location
once during this time), and it houses only a few of the women
we support, most of whom live in rooms they rent. Only the
very neediest ladies become residents, and during the time of
my visit, it was home to just six women. Two of these ladies are
elderly and unable to work; the other four have various mental health challenges. WWR's offices are on the second floor,
where Esther works with her gentle colleague Nina, and it is
where our committee meets.

Once I had switched my dusty outdoor shoes for plastic
slip-ons, all of us made our way to the top floor and the meeting room. The ladies moved at various speeds, and since they
had two flights of stairs to climb, it took a while before we
were all seated: some on wicker seats, others on the floor. Over
the next hour, we sang Christian worship songs, prayed, and
Esther shared a short message. The ladies sang in Nepali, and if
I recognized the song, I would join in in English; I am hopeless

at remembering lyrics, though, so I often just hummed or clapped along. A favourite of the ladies is 'This is the Day',[2] and I have often sung it with them; the lyrics are simple, which is a great relief.

This particular Thursday was Thanksgiving in the USA, and since I had been living in Alabama, USA before moving to Nepal, I continued the American tradition and asked each of them to name something they were thankful for. I told them how grateful I was that I had met Eileen many years ago and that God had brought me back to live in Nepal, close to them. I had intended for this time to be one of joy, but as each lady shared how WWR had turned her life around, there were more and more tears. I started to wonder if I had done the right thing by asking them to talk about themselves, but Esther assured me this was a good time for them as most of them, despite living with each other 24/7, had not heard each other's stories. I can only assume that this indicates the amount of shame they feel about their pasts.

Throughout all this time, both Esther and Tanya translated for me. At just 26 years of age, Tanya is the youngest resident in the home and is positively vibrant compared to the others. She encouraged each lady to speak and gently teased them if they would not. In the process, she made everyone in the room laugh.

I first met Tanya two years ago on one of my brief trips back to Nepal. Esther and I had visited a partner organization of ours, called Koshish, and she had also stood out then. Koshish is a self-help organization that was founded by a Christian man called Matrika. He had experienced depression and mental torment in his twenties, eventually leading him to attempt suicide. Mercifully, his attempt failed, and upon realizing God had other plans for him, he founded Koshish. In the beginning, the organization rescued men and women who had been thrown out of their homes, or chained up within them, and had severe mental health problems. Koshish was the first organization to do this in Nepal, and at times Matrika's phone would ring incessantly with requests to rescue people from every district of Nepal. It became so overwhelming that, on more than one occasion, he had to change his phone number. Nowadays, Koshish's work is focused on advocacy and advice, and Matrika has increasing influence within the Ministry of Health, whom he lobbies to care for all Nepalis with psychosocial issues.

Koshish supports WWR by providing free advice to us if any of the women we assist experience mental health problems. In return, we now support some of the women that Koshish has rescued and rehabilitated but whose families will not welcome them home. In 2018 Tanya had already spent six months being cared for by Koshish and was a resident at their rehabilitation home for women. She was an oasis of calm among the other residents and sat with Esther, Matrika and me in the courtyard of the hostel to talk about her future, in English. While we chatted, the other residents of the home edged closer to us, curious to know what we were discussing. Since many of them had been living on the streets, their heads had been shaved to rid them of lice and fleas. One woman, who had newly been rescued, roamed among us all, attempting to pull the hair of those who still had it and spitting at everyone. She was followed closely by some of the Koshish staff members, who did their best to lovingly rein her in. I do not doubt that in developed nations, a different approach would likely be taken regarding the help and rehabilitation of women with these kinds of problems. They probably would not be able to mix like this for fear of traumatizing or triggering each other. In Nepal, however, where so many are considered unworthy of help, Koshish's rehabilitation home affords a huge improvement in their circumstances, and it is the best that resources allow.

There were also young toddlers and babies among our conversation spectators and eavesdroppers. Many of the women that Koshish rescues arrive pregnant or have recently given birth. Tragically, homeless women are frequently raped on the streets of Nepal. Usually, homeless men are the perpetrators, and sometimes women exchange their bodies for food, but it is always heartless and cruel. Another degradation forced upon women that no one else appears to care for.

As we talked together, Matrika and Tanya shared their hopes for her future. Matrika had noticed that she was bright and able to speak English. Since she had not had the opportunity to finish her schooling, he wondered if WWR could house her and pay for her to continue her education so that she could complete her School Leaving Certificate (SLC, similar to the UK's GCSE). If she had taken up her studies while staying at their rehabilitation home, it is likely the other residents would have destroyed her books.

At this time, Tanya was unwilling to say much about her past, and Matrika warned us that doing so could upset her as it was still very traumatic for her. He gave us brief details of her condition; she had been diagnosed by them as having bi-polar disorder and experienced extreme mood swings between mania and depression. Knowing that Koshish would continue to support her treatment and would advise WWR's staff on how best to look after her, we were pleased to agree that Tanya could move to our women's home, and we began the process of finding a school for her.

During the past two years, from the time Tanya moved to WWR's home to today, there have been both challenges and delights. Her moods have been taxing for our staff, and at times she has refused to go to school; it has taken all the patience of both our carers and Koshish's to keep her education going. During her periods of mania, she has stayed out all night, and we have not known where she was. Despite all these complications, she completed her SLC and scored a B+, a remarkable achievement.

Now, here I was two years later, singing and praying with Tanya and hearing her recount parts of her story. She was especially grateful to WWR's staff members, who had stuck with her despite her mood swings, and she recognized that the opportunity to go back to school, and not being forced into some kind of menial work, gave her hope for the future. She had also become a Christian during the intervening years, even getting baptized, which is a brave step for Nepali converts to take, and I was keen to know how her conversion had occurred.

Following the time of worship, together the two of us recorded a short video for her sponsor in the USA (WWR offers donors the chance to sponsor a woman) using my mobile phone; this was only possible because she speaks excellent English. Her sponsor told me later that she loved and appreciated seeing the two of us together and hearing Tanya tell parts of her own story.

For lunch, Tanya proudly prepared *rotis*, a traditional flat bread, for everyone and described how Dolma, the oldest woman living at the home, had been teaching her to cook. The two of them and Nina formed a production line in the kitchen, and we were all treated to spicy vegetables and as many *chapatis*, a roti made with *atta*/wheat flour, as we could eat. It was clear that Tanya is the home's social butterfly and, though there are times when she can be difficult, spending time with her was never dull. Over lunch, the ladies discussed their histories further. I suppose that not having heard each other's circumstances in detail before, they all wanted to ask follow-up questions. Tanya said that she had no father, and there was a hilarious moment when Gyanu, a straightlaced older lady, quipped that Tanya's mother could not have done it on her own. Everyone burst out laughing.

To firmly cement her position as the home's extrovert, after lunch, Tanya treated us to an impromptu dance display. While still seated on benches around the kitchen table, we watched her dance to a stream of music from Bollywood tunes to Nepali folk songs and everything in-between. Some of the other ladies took turns to join her, and she directed their moves, telling them what to do with their arms and when to switch places with her in the routines. By the end of it, I felt as if I had been out to my very own dinner and dance spectacle; good food, good company and wonderful entertainment. I could not have asked for a better lunchtime.

There was still a lot I did not know about Tanya, and so I asked if I could interview her. Thankfully, she agreed, and I made plans to visit her the following week. Esther would be away for a night at a wedding, so I would need to find my way to the women's home alone and rely on Tanya's excellent, but in some ways limited, English. As I walked home that day, Esther and I stopped to take photos of every turning and intersection on the way; these would be guideposts to help me return a week later.

When I arrived at the women's home five days later, I was in a much better mood. The traffic along my way had been just as blaring as before, but I was excited to spend time with Tanya and hear more from her. Within minutes of my arrival, we both made our way up to the meeting room on the top floor, quickly this time, and sat down next to each other.

I reminded Tanya of when I first met her with Matrika at Koshish and how thrilled I was to be speaking to her now. She did not remember our meeting which, if I am honest, hurt a little. My pride had assumed that I should be one of the heroes of her story, but that was not to be the case. I showed her a photo of our first meeting, but since I was behind the camera, I was not pictured in it. Instead, Esther, Matrika and an empty chair for me were there. I hoped it would jog her memory and she might remember me as the foreigner who talked to her that day; there is nothing particularly memorable about me, but I do not expect she has the chance to talk to many British people. She still did not remember, and as I was to find out during our subsequent conversation, there was a lot that Tanya could not recall.

Focusing on what Tanya could remember, I asked her how she had ended up at Koshish, and she told me she had run away while in tenth grade when she was around 15 years old. She had drifted among the streets of Bhat Bhateni and Naxal, both areas of central Kathmandu, begging for food. In her words, Tanya stated that she 'couldn't recognize anyone' while on the streets and was completely isolated despite the masses of people around her. Esther told me subsequently that many homeless people in Nepal wear nothing below their waists (though perhaps the top part of their *kurta* may drop low enough to cover their privates) and Tanya had confirmed to her that she too had only been half-dressed during this time. Tipped off by Tanya's relatives and asked to intervene, Koshish had rescued her from the streets of Kathmandu and brought her to their rehabilitation home.

Going back further in her life, I wanted to understand why Tanya had run away from her home to begin with. She told me about the fateful day that her aunt told her that Tanya's mother was not her birth mother. Tanya insisted that her aunt had told her because she believed she had a right to know the truth. The story goes that Tanya's uncle found a baby abandoned in a pile of waste and asked his sister, Tanya's mother, to take care of her. Tanya grew up believing that her mother was her birth mother, but when Tanya became a teenager and was difficult to handle, her mother began to push her away. So, Tanya's aunt stepped in, perhaps motivated by a desire to explain her mother's behaviour and hoping Tanya might be more grateful for her mother's kindness which was, after all, given to an orphaned Tanya unwarranted. Instead, the news triggered a massive emotional breakdown in Tanya that caused her to run away and become unrecognizable to herself.

At this moment in our conversation, purely by coincidence, Tanya's phone rang and another of her aunts, one she described as loving her very much, was on the other end. Tanya quickly told her aunt that she was busy and would call back later, but this interruption prompted Tanya to show me some photos of her family on her phone. First, I saw her aunts, dressed in bright blue saris for a wedding; they look a little uncomfortable so dressed up, but appear friendly and dignified. I was puzzled because her mother was not with them. Next, we looked at the only photo Tanya has of her mother, who has not welcomed her home since her teenage years. In this photo, her mother looks sullen and troubled; though it is hard to tell, it would not surprise me if her mother suffered from some kind of mental illness too, such is the way that she appears to be withdrawn from her surroundings. I wondered what the truth about Tanya's parentage was.

Tanya's narrative jumped again, and she told me about the three years she spent in Dhading. It seems that WWR was not the first organization that Koshish approached to help her and secure her future. According to Tanya, it was suggested that she work for an American man and his Nepali wife who ran a small guest house and mountain trekking company that caters for tourists. Given her aptitude for English, it should have been a good fit for her skills. While there, she carried out all sorts of domestic work at the guest house and, in return, received board and lodging. She was in Dhading when the massive 2015 earthquake shook Nepal, and many lives were lost; thankfully, she and the other staff were outdoors at the time, and no one was injured. Her time at Dhading ended in more heartbreak when frustratingly, she was accused of inappropriately touching a male co-worker who was a little older than her. While the American man was away, the Nepali woman punished her with a beating.

Tanya ran away again. Following the thrashing, she waited until midnight and departed in the dark with not a single rupee, having not been paid in cash while she worked at the lodge. This time she knew where to go and headed directly for Koshish back in Kathmandu, a journey of fifty miles. She understood that once there, she would receive food, a warm welcome and that she would be safe. Describing this incident to me, she said it was her proudest moment. She knows that she did the right thing and did not stay any longer to put up with the lies and abuse. It was just a few months later that she met Esther and me and came to live at WWR's home. At several points in our conversation, she told me that we were brilliant because we gave her pocket money.

By now, I was curious to know how Tanya became a Christian. She told me that on arriving at our women's home, she thought 'oh no' because she wanted to remain a Buddhist, and everyone was a Christian. However, when she experienced a bout of stomach pain and fever, she thought it might be sensible to check if Jesus was really there, and so she prayed to him to heal her. He did, and she felt good believing in him and being with the other women who were Christian. Another of the home's residents went to Pishon River Church in Baghdol, and so she decided to accompany her on the bus journey to get there. Once she had experienced worship and had talked to other Christians, she soon decided to get baptized. She told me that she has been 'running with Jesus for two years now', and that seems a great way to describe her faith. I sensed that if she were ever to run away again, Jesus would be right beside her.

Tanya also credited God with gifting her the ability to communicate in English. When I asked her how she came to be so good at English, she offered another convoluted history. Perhaps it was the boarding school she was sent to at age 4; she had not mentioned this before, or the other five schools she attended as a child, though she could not explain why she went to so many schools. She also said that she taught herself English by watching TV and reading newspapers. I wondered out loud if she had much chance to practise English with the tourists in Dhading, but she informed me that she was not allowed to talk to them.

I wanted to know what Tanya would like to achieve in the future. She was studying for her 'plus 2' exams (rather like British A-levels) in six subjects and was proud of the sports medals for football and volleyball that she had won at school. She told me she liked to play in defensive positions and was good at guarding the goal.

Like most of us, her Facebook page records the history of her greatest achievements and best moments. She is only able to use Facebook because she managed to save a small amount, which was matched by Matrika so that she could purchase a smartphone. Another accomplishment to be proud of. Once again, she mentioned how grateful she was for the pocket money WWR provided her.

Was marriage a possibility? Tanya believes that Nepali women face many injustices, such as acid attacks and rape, the dowry system and little independence. In addition, she noted that many people in Nepal think negatively about Christians, but she knows God listens to and solves problems. She related a news story about a woman who was recently set on fire because her husband's family was dissatisfied with the dowry her family provided. As a result, Tanya did not want, or expect, to get married and intended to provide for herself. Her ideal job was to work in a supermarket as a receptionist offering a warm welcome to customers, using both her Nepali and English language skills. All supermarkets are considered upmarket in Nepal and consequently employ more staff than they might in the UK.

Tanya's biggest obstacle to this dream is Nepal's citizenship laws. Currently, she does not have a birth certificate or citizenship papers. Without these, she cannot be employed easily nor own land. It is fair to say that obtaining citizenship for each of WWR's ladies has been one of the biggest challenges that we have had to face over the years. For decades, obtaining a birth certificate or citizenship paper was only possible for a woman if her father or husband were present; in some cases, a brother could step in (for instance, in Lila's case). These patriarchal requirements were changed in the late 1990s, and legally a woman is now permitted to obtain these documents for herself. Yet, in practice, women can rarely do this, and low-level bureaucrats refuse to complete the necessary paperwork to authorize citizenship without a man present. Many hours of both Esther's and Nina's time has been spent in cramped offices waiting for obstinate men, still upset with the new law, to approve and stamp the necessary documents.

Since Tanya was once homeless, there is a loophole for street-dwellers that should allow her to obtain citizenship, but so far, she has had no success. At the end of my interview with her, we prayed that the process would be expedited.

Before I left the women's home, Nina insisted on feeding me. This time the lunch was *roti* and chips, which were rather too many carbohydrates for me. No matter, they kept me going on the long walk home, which this time was much more pleasant as I identified a winding path on Google maps that avoided the main roads. It turned out that I passed through fields belonging to an agricultural college. There were groups of students in white lab coats tending crops which made for a bizarre sight.

As I reflected on my time with Tanya, I realized how many questions I still had. Can a brother tell his sister to raise a baby he has found in the garbage? Why was Tanya's mother never married? Might Tanya be her uncle's child? Perhaps the result of an illegitimate affair. Why did it fall to her aunt to tell her that she was not her mother's daughter? I felt confused. Similarly, the incident at Dhading puzzled me; when she was accused of inappropriate touching, why was the boy's word taken over hers? There were so many details missing from her story; Tanya had been unable to tell me how she fed and looked after herself while living on the streets of Kathmandu, and her journey back from Dhading to Kathmandu was similarly vague; all she could say was that she got a lift with strangers. How did this come about in the middle of the night? Every time I asked follow-up questions, she couldn't provide any further specifics.

A day or two later, Esther returned from the wedding she had attended, and we had lunch together at a roof-top restaurant overlooking the world heritage site at Patan Durbar Square, no more than half a mile from my house. Esther had an interesting connection to the place; next to us was a dilapidated building that had been Esther's secondary school. Before becoming a school, it had been a palace, and Esther told me about the huge archway through its middle that had been built to allow elephants to enter. How I wish I had been able to visit Nepal then and had seen princes riding elephants.

I told Esther about my bewilderment with parts of Tanya's story, and she, too, admitted confusion. Some of the details she was aware of contradicted what I had been told, and she believed Tanya had only spent three months, not three years, in Dhading. I began to despair about how I would write up Tanya's story. The discrepancies seemed to keep on mounting up.

I returned to England for Christmas and had to spend another couple of weeks in quarantine, during which time I planned to write out Tanya's story. Each Sunday, I had a regular prayer time over Zoom with my friend in Alabama who sponsors Tanya and for whom the two of us had made the video. I shared with her that I felt hopeless about ever making sense of Tanya's story, and she prayed with me. That night, it suddenly became clear to me. The confusion I was experiencing is exactly how Tanya feels all the time. Her mental health problems have caused sporadic memory loss, and she cannot rely on her own recollection of events. When she discovered that her mother and family had been lying to her about her birth, everything she had presumed to be true and had clung to was removed from her.

Tanya has been tossed about on the waves of her unreliable memory all her life, and those that could have provided a safe harbour disappeared when she needed them most. She did not know who to trust. As I reflected on this and prayed for her, I resolved that as much as we could, neither I nor WWR would ever lie to her or let her down. Thankfully, I know it is not all down to me, and I am immensely grateful that she has found Jesus. I pray that he will always be the anchor that her soul so desperately needs.

3

Lover: Somi

The Covid pandemic still had plenty of twists and turns in store for me. Having returned to England for Christmas to see Zach and Beth, I became stuck there when British scientists detected a new Covid variant. Nepal's government acted swiftly and closed its borders to all British travellers, even those that lived there. I spent January living with my welcoming parents, who by this time had also got used to the ups and downs of overseas postings with the army, and I began to feel a little like a teenager living at home again. I didn't know when I would be able to return to Nepal. Would it be after weeks or months? I missed Simon, Esther, Tanya and all WWR's ladies so much. I had already spent sixteen years waiting to return to them after my last stint living in Kathmandu; my indefinite wait for Nepal's government to ease travel restrictions was excruciating.

Meanwhile, in Kathmandu, Covid-19 was not the only disruption. Right before Christmas, on Sunday 20 December, when I was already in the UK, Nepal's prime minister, K.P. Sharma Oli asked the president to dissolve the house of representatives, Nepal's parliament. Fresh elections were called for April and May 2021. Thus began a new phase of protests and unrest in the capital. When I eventually arrived back in Kathmandu in early February, a massive demonstration blocked my route home. Irate crowds had gathered outside the century-old Singha Durbar (Lion's Palace), which is now home to Nepal's government. The Rana family built Singha Durbar for themselves after having installed themselves as hereditary prime ministers in 1846. They placed the king and his family under house arrest until the 1950s, while they took all the responsibility and rewards of ruling Nepal.

The roads and open spaces around Singha Durbar have been the focus of many protests and uprisings. In each decade of the last century, the calls for democracy in Nepal have become louder and louder. This time around, there are members of political parties calling for secular communism, and opposing them are supporters of the former king, who wish for him to be reinstalled, and for Nepal to revert to being a Hindu kingdom. As a result, the vehicle carrying me from the airport was forced to take to the back roads. Thankfully, I arrived home safely, and for the next week, while in quarantine, it was the familiar sound of noisy crows that woke me each day from my jetlagged sleep.

Back in November, before my trip home for Christmas, Somi's wedding had been just days away. I had sent some money to help her pay for the wedding expenses and to assist her with setting up a new room for her and her husband. Prior to the wedding, Somi both lived and worked at WWR's women's home, Mahima Griha, preparing meals for the residents and keeping the place clean. As a married woman, she would live elsewhere but continue to run things at the women's home. Both Esther and I had prayed for her as we knew she was making a difficult decision by choosing to marry someone who wasn't a Christian. Somi already had a son, though he was undocumented, having neither a birth certificate nor citizenship. Her new husband had promised to arrange a birth certificate for her son after their marriage.

As I made my way to the WWR's women's home to interview Somi, I passed through groups of armed police gathered at my local intersection. Simon and I had also seen them the day before, blocking vehicle access to the main road through our area. It turns out that a female undergraduate had been killed in a road traffic accident. The police were there to oversee her angry classmates and outraged students from across Lalitpur, who had gathered to protest and call on Nepal's government to improve road safety. I walked on, saddened that such a heavy-handed response from the police was necessary. Since Christmas, it seemed that protest and unrest were closer at hand than they had been before.

It was fantastic to see Somi again. She is extraordinarily thin, which does concern me as I never seem to see her eat, but she appears to possess an endless supply of patience and energy for everything that goes on at the women's home. She hails from the Tamang ethnic group, which is one of the hill tribes. She has high cheekbones that are common to people of this ethnicity; her features are pretty stunning. As we talked, she insisted on sitting on the floor and seemed quite comfortable there even though our conversation lasted for hours.

Somi grew up in a village in the district of Sindulpalchowk; this region borders Kathmandu to the south and butts up to Tibet in the north. The most commonly used mountain pass from Tibet into Nepal passes through this area. Consequently, the indigenous people bear a strong resemblance to their Tibetan neighbours, and for generations, Tibetan Buddhism has been a heavy influence. Her village contained a *Gumba*, a white dome-like *stupa*, and a small monastery where a maroon-clad monk resided. The village residents formed a committee to maintain the *Gumba* and organize festivals. Though her family attended these, they were not involved in the committee, and their belief in Buddhism was nominal. Somi's family were poor, and despite owning land, it remained uncultivated.

There were five children in Somi's family. She was the middle one, with both an older sister and brother and a younger sister and brother. As she told me this, she laughed at the perfect symmetry; like all middle girls, she was known to her family as Maili. It is unusual for siblings in Nepal to call each other by their first names; instead, they use terms such as *Dai* (older brother) or *Bahini* (younger sister). Even among the Gurkha wives that I mix with at the British Camp, they refer to each other using these familiar names, though they are not related. The custom originates from a superstitious belief that speaking a child's name aloud would identify them to evil spirits, as I have mentioned earlier.

Though impoverished, it seems as if Somi's childhood was a normal and relatively happy one. Her older brother left for Kathmandu in his late teens and lived there with his cousins and their family. While there, he and his cousins converted to Christianity through Gyaneshwar Church (which Lila also attended). He told no one back home in the village that he had become a Christian as it was viewed as both a *bideshi-dharma* (foreign religion) and suitable only for low-caste people who were regarded as greedy and just converted to get money. During *Dashain*, Nepal's main festival, he would visit either before or after the celebration days to avoid receiving *tikas* from his family. These blessings are conferred on prescribed days, but he remained in Kathmandu away from his family to avoid offending them by refusing the *tikas* and revealing his new Christian faith.

Tragedy befell Somi's older sister at the age of 15; she tumbled over and became paralyzed. Heartbreakingly, she was to spend the next five years confined to her bed, which meant Somi had to help out more at home. In 1999, by the time her sister was 20 years old, Somi's older brother had gained more confidence in his new-found faith and had begun to speak openly about the gospel while visiting their village. However, the only response he received was rejection. Together with his 'sister-cousin',[3] they offered to pray for Somi's bed-bound sister. There was no sudden miracle, but three nights later, her sister had a vision of Jesus, and he told her to stand. According to Somi, the following morning her sister was able to 'crawl like a cow', and soon after, she was walking. To this day, Somi's sister still has some problems with her hands and feet, but she is now married to a church leader and has a daughter.

Somi's family were overawed by the miraculous healing and pretty much became Christians on the spot. The whole village was similarly impressed, and a new church was born. Initially, the congregation met under a plastic sheet where they sat on dry leaves, but Somi's father soon donated one *ropani* of land (equal to sixteen *aana*, or one-eighth of an acre) on which a church could be built. The village banded together to raise funds to erect a church building, and Somi remembers donating everything she earned that season (5,000 NRs worth £35) from working in the fields towards the construction project. The healings continued, and villagers were set free from leprosy and other illnesses. Being a Christian was now acceptable in the village, and Somi confirms that the Ghortali Issa Mandali (Ghortali Jesus Church) is still going strong today, with 100 members from every caste, including Dalits. Sadly, the first building was destroyed in the 2015 earthquake, but it has been rebuilt on the same land that her father donated.

Another consequence of Somi's sister's vision of Jesus and conversion to Christianity was that she now insisted Somi should go to school. She felt strongly that Somi should not have to sign using her thumbprint, as many of WWR's illiterate women do, and should be able to read and write. Having not attended school until this point, Somi joined Class 2 at the age of 12. She spent the next four years in school, typically alternating between fifteen days of work in the fields and fifteen days in the classroom. She had no pen and no books, so she sold fruit to afford these.

Since childhood, Somi has dreamed of flying in a plane, and she still longs to travel. While visiting her elder brother and cousins in Jorpati, an area in the north-east of Kathmandu where many Tamang live, she met a well-dressed broker who told her that if she went abroad, she would earn a lot of money. Somi remembers this woman clearly; she had long nails, long hair and wore a beautiful sari. Evidently, her appearance made a big impression on Somi. The broker told Somi, and five other girls living in Jorpati at that time, that if they successfully applied for their passports, she would arrange jobs for them to work in Japan. The broker asked for 1 lakh rupees (worth £700) from each of them to organize their new employment. Somi sold her gold jewellery to raise half a lakh and borrowed the other half from a local man who charged interest on the loan.

Early in the morning on a given date, the broker asked the girls to meet her in Bhaktapur Durbar Square. There are three Durbar squares in the Kathmandu Valley, in each of the three old cities, all of which are world heritage sites. They contain buildings that display the highest quality of Nepali architecture. The girls met the broker in the open plaza in front of the temples and palaces and handed over the money, full of excitement that the following week they would be travelling to Japan. By the end of the day, though, they realized they had been duped. The broker could not be contacted, and since they had not met her at an office to which they could return, it was impossible to track her down.

Somi returned to her village feeling terribly stressed about the money she now owed. She lied to her parents and told them that she had left her gold jewellery with her sister in Kathmandu for safe-keeping. She thinks her father saw through her lie, but her mum believed her. By working in the fields surrounding her village, she earnt enough to pay off the interest on her loan, yet she wasn't able to reduce the capital amount. Even now, she is fiercely independent. She took full responsibility for her naïve mistake and didn't ask anyone to bail her out by paying off her loan.

Six months later, Somi heard about another work placement; this time, the job was in Saudi Arabia. Her desire to work abroad was even more potent now because she needed the increased income to pay off her loan. Back in Jorpati again, she met with a relative of her sister's landlord who told her that she could work in the Middle East if she paid a 60,000 NRs (£420) arrangement charge. I asked Somi what made her trust this agent, given that the other broker had stolen from her. It seems there were several reasons to trust him. Firstly, this agent was compassionate and gave her a 10,000 NRs discount on his fee; he also paid for her to undergo a medical assessment and he was able to tell her the name of the hospital where she would be working in Saudi Arabia. Already in debt, Somi borrowed 50,000 NRs from her sister's landlord, though this time no interest was due.

In recent weeks, I had read in one of Kathmandu's newspapers that Nepal's government was considering making it mandatory for women under the age of 40 to obtain a man's permission (father, husband or brother) before leaving the country. The proposal has rightly been derided online for its sexist and patriarchal overtones, but in my view, it is attempting to address a genuine problem. It's thought that up to

200,000 Nepali women and girls are currently overseas having been trafficked. Of course, the government's efforts should be focused on cracking down on the traffickers rather than penalizing all women. Still, I empathize with their desire to do something to stop this horrific trade. Thankfully, Somi did not become a trafficking victim, but she was very fortunate not to have become enslaved far from home, given her vulnerability and desperation.

Having given the agent the money and her passport, Somi was caught up in a whirl of excitement as the subsequent events happened quickly. She was issued a visa to work in Saudi Arabia within a week, and three days after that, she flew there. During the intervening days, she had to purchase a suitcase and clothes, for which she took another loan. She also needed to say goodbye to her parents. When she departed from them at her village, she didn't tell them she was headed to Saudi Arabia. Instead, she pretended she was simply returning to Kathmandu. To avoid bursting into tears, she didn't look at their faces as the bus drove away; by now, they were used to her comings and goings and had no idea of her imminent journey.

Somi travelled to Saudi Arabia with fifteen other young Nepalis; she was one of seven women. As she described her first flight on a plane, her face beamed. She loved sitting comfortably in the plane, and before it took off, she called all her friends to tell them she was onboard. When the noisy engines began and the plane taxied to the end of the runway, she tightened her seatbelt as much as she could. I'm glad she was given a window seat, and once in the air, she delightedly looked down on the familiar sights of Kathmandu. No flight over the Himalayas passes without turbulence, but she told me she was brave and didn't scream. Another surprise was the food onboard; she hadn't thought about what she would eat or drink during the flight and didn't know a meal would be served. She remembered that the food was 'VIP standard' on the way to Saudi Arabia and knew precisely what it was: a chicken curry. A foreigner sat next to her was asleep and didn't touch their food; Somi thought that was such decadence – she ate every morsel of hers. Sadly, the food on her flight home was nowhere near as good; perhaps the novelty of plane food had worn off by then.

When the group landed in Riyadh, Saudi men collected them from the airport, where they met up with another group of newly arrived migrant workers. Somi's first night on Saudi soil was spent sleeping on the floor of a large room, from which they were not allowed to leave, and to which their meals were delivered. She had taken along her Bible, and when she got it out to read in the morning, another believer from Dharan made herself known to her. Somi was grateful there was another Christian with her.

Everything the agent had promised Somi came true; mercifully, her decision to trust him was proved correct. She began working as a cleaner at the King Khaled Hospital in Najran and earned 650 Saudi Riyals (worth 18,000 NRs then, or £126) per month. After a week, her supervisor noticed that she was small and fast, and switched her role to a porter. This was an excellent swap for Somi because, as a porter, she spent her days with the hospital's wealthy patients who tipped generously. One elderly woman insisted on giving her 500 Riyals, though Somi tried to protest, worried that accepting the tip might be perceived as taking advantage of an aged patient. Spending time with the patients also gave Somi a chance to learn Arabic, and astonishingly, she claims she picked up the language in just a fortnight. To demonstrate, she said *'Salaam alaikum'* to me, to show how polite and respectful she was.

Life in Saudi Arabia for a migrant worker sounds exceptionally regimented. She lived at a hostel for women, and each day, a bus that was solely for female migrants would pick the workers up and take them to the hospital for their shifts. They were not allowed to walk to the hospital, although it wasn't that far away. The other migrants came from Pakistan, India and Bangladesh, though unsurprisingly, she spent most of her time with Nepalis since it was easier to chat in their mother tongue. She teamed up with three other Nepali friends to cook together and share chores. Each fortnight a bus collected them and took them to the bazaar to buy food and clothes; this was the only time she could leave the hostel other than for work. On weekends, they washed their uniforms, played with their phones and gossiped, unable to do anything else. Still, she has no complaints about the restrictions she lived under.

There were CCTV cameras everywhere at the bazaar, and Somi recounts an incident when a Bangladeshi man stole some plates and spoons. Bright lights flashed, and he was quickly arrested before spending three nights in jail. Following that, he worked for a further month to pay off his debt for the stolen items and was then promptly repatriated to Bangladesh. Clearly, Somi felt under surveillance even during her downtime.

All of the workers eagerly anticipated their trips to the bazaar; it was the only time they could talk to men from their home countries who were also in Saudi Arabia as migrant workers. After six months in the country, Somi began meeting up with one particular Nepali man, a driver from a faraway city, who became her boyfriend. She smiled as she recalls the gifts he bought her and the attention he lavished upon her. Knowing that she was in Saudi Arabia because she owed money, he offered to pay back her loans so that she could return to Nepal sooner. However, Somi insisted that she would pay them back herself.

After two years of meeting up every other weekend in Saudi Arabia, they arranged to return to Nepal together. Somi did not tell her family she was back in the country; instead, the two of them rented a single room together in Chabahil, Kathmandu. They spent a month alone in each other's company before her boyfriend returned to Saudi Arabia to continue working there. According to Somi, she knew nothing about how babies are made, and she asserts they had sex only once.

Once he was back in Saudi Arabia, she told him on the phone that she had missed two of her periods. Given that she didn't know what that meant, he informed her that she was pregnant. The secrecy continued; Somi told no one about her pregnancy but did have a check-up at the hospital, where they confirmed her due date. Her boyfriend was happy about the baby and told her it was his child, not to 'throw it' and that he would take another holiday from work when it was due.

Only four months later, when Somi was six months pregnant, there was dreadful news. Her boyfriend had been drink-driving in Saudi Arabia and had suffered a heart attack while at the wheel. His car had collided with another, and he had died. When Somi heard the news, she was understandably devastated. She still had told no one of her pregnancy, and now her family would undoubtedly view the child as illegitimate.

Not knowing what to do, Somi left Chabahil and returned to her village. Since she was thin, she could hide her baby bump under layers of clothing, and no one suspected she was pregnant. While in Kathmandu, following her boyfriend's death, she had begun drinking alcohol. She continued this habit in secret while back in the village.

As the due date neared, she became more and more distraught and started to believe that suicide was her only option. She packed a small bag and told her parents she was going back to Kathmandu to see her brother. Early one morning, her father took her to the bus park and attempted to give her

500 NRs; she refused, knowing it would be wasted if she went through with her plan. After boarding the bus, she began sipping from a bottle of *raksi*, locally brewed alcohol that is commonplace in the hills where Janajati hill tribes predominate. Formerly known as *matwalis*, literally 'alcohol drinkers', these tribes' brewing and alcohol consumption initially caused high caste Hindus from Kathmandu to rank them as less pure than themselves.

Rather than travelling to Kathmandu, Somi got off at the next bazaar and, in her drunken haze, wandered towards the river. I had heard this part of the story before, and in my mind, I had imagined a wide river with gentle riverbanks, such as the ones I am familiar with in Britain. Of course, rivers in Nepal are nothing like this. They are usually at the bottom of deep gorges, and Somi's plan was to jump off the precipice into the churning river below. Miraculously, at that moment, she heard a voice telling her not to jump. There was no one around, so she knows it was God who called out to her at that instant. He spoke again: 'Don't jump.' Praise God that she obeyed him.

By now, she was very drunk, and she collapsed back onto a large rock. She couldn't get up, and in time she lost consciousness. Passengers on a local bus spotted her and came to her rescue. She doesn't know exactly what happened, but when she woke up, she found herself in a local hospital with two saline drips attached to her arms.

A doctor informed Somi that her baby had already done a stool in her womb, and they must deliver the baby by caesarean section as soon as possible. There was no operating theatre at this rural hospital, so the only option was to send Somi to the maternity hospital in Kathmandu by ambulance. Somi refused and told the doctor she wanted to die. Mercifully, Somi's small set of belongings had accompanied her to the hospital. When the Christian doctor saw the Bible, she encouraged Somi to put her life in God's hands.

It was late afternoon when she arrived at the maternity hospital. There was paperwork to complete; Somi gave a false name and refused to give any next-of-kin details. She signed the consent form for the operation herself as she refused to contact anyone who could look after her while at the hospital. At midnight, her son was delivered.

Somi remained in the hospital for one week, surrounded by other new mothers and their families; it was clear to them all that no one was visiting her, and the father of her son was absent. Since Somi's own father had waved her off at the village and she hadn't arrived at her brother's home, her family had reported her missing to the police. The woman in the next bed to Somi told her she must contact her family to let them know she was alright. So finally, she called her brother and bravely told him she was in the maternity hospital having given birth. His response was not anger; he just cried and called off the police search. During the following week, he visited the hospital three times to find his younger sister, but since Somi had given a false name, he couldn't trace her.

As the news that Somi had given birth to a boy spread through her family and village, a false assumption also circulated. Given that Somi had been working in Saudi Arabia, it was rumoured that her child's father was a Saudi man who had taken advantage of her. She did not contradict this theory and kept the lie going even when she joined WWR. It was not until three years later that I was informed that the father was, in fact, Nepali.

As I thought back to my own fragile state of mind after giving birth, I was stunned by the events that followed. During the week Somi was in the hospital, two people offered to buy

Somi's son from her. The first was a doctor, who said they could both live with her for ten days while Somi recovered from her C-section. After that, the doctor would raise the boy as her own, and Somi would need to move out, but the doctor would help her find a hospital job. The second offer came via a nurse-scout who was on the lookout within the hospital for unwanted babies. She informed an adoption agent that an unplanned and fatherless baby had been born. Horrifyingly, the agent visited Somi in the ward, and the sum of 1 lakh (£700) was offered for her son. Thankfully, it is illegal in Nepal to offer money to mothers for their children, but this didn't stop the nurse and agent from trying to take advantage of Somi's vulnerable condition.

I am thrilled to write that there was a third visitor to Somi's bedside. This woman was Hitu, who attended Gyaneshwar Church with Somi's older sister (the paralyzed woman who had been healed). Hitu is a kind and matronly woman; at that time, WWR employed her to run Anugraha Ashram (Grace Women's Home) on the gentle slopes of Kathmandu Valley's rim. When Hitu had given birth at Patan Hospital in the late 1980s, her husband had not bothered to collect her and bring her home because she had given birth to a girl. Hitu knew what it was like to have no one to turn to.

Hitu told Somi that her son was a gift from God and that he would need his mother. She invited Somi to come and live at Anugraha Ashram and convinced the doctors that WWR would take good care of her. By this time, Somi had begun to become attached to her son and wanted to take responsibility for him. She told the doctor, 'I will do this', and agreed with Hitu that she would try Anugraha Ashram for six months. Somi told me that before arriving at Anugraha Ashram, she felt as if she was the only victim in the world, and no one had suffered like her. On meeting the other residents, she discovered they had each experienced trauma. She felt comforted knowing they didn't judge her and would support her.

Two days later, an event occurred that bound the residents together even more. In April 2015, a massive earthquake shook Nepal, which I have mentioned before. I have a photo of Somi and her son taken a few hours after the quake. She looks like a child herself, and her son is tiny, swaddled in her arms. There is a clear look of shock and fear on her face. I can't imagine how she must have felt; in the space of three months, she had lost her boyfriend, whom she loved, given birth to an unplanned baby and survived an earthquake. She told me she could do nothing but hold her son and repeat 'hallelujah' over and over again. I asked if she felt worried about her parents and whether they had survived the earthquake, but she said she was incapable of contacting them. Overwhelmed with emotion and unable to think straight, it was all she could do to hold on to her son.

The next three years passed relatively uneventfully. Somi settled into the rhythm of life at Anugraha Ashram and began the process of healing while helping with the animals, crops and kitchen. Meanwhile, her son grew into a healthy toddler. In 2018, faced with the rising cost of running Anugraha Ashram, the other trustees and I made the difficult decision to close it. We relocated the women to a smaller house, which we named Mahima Griha, where the ladies now live; it is far closer to Kathmandu in a built-up area. Though we felt it was a real step down in the quality of life WWR offered the women, it turned out they were happy to be near shops, their churches and bus routes. God knew what he was doing when he led us down this challenging path.

Hitu decided she didn't want to relocate with the women, which was entirely understandable, given that she had lived and worked at the same place for the last seven years; it was time for her to have a break. Somi was one of the few women who could read and write and keep basic accounts. She also enjoyed looking after the older ladies and impressed us with her energy, so we appointed her to replace Hitu when Mahima Griha opened. I love that she has come full circle and is now in a position to aid and rescue other women who may find themselves in a similar position to herself, and Hitu before her. She embodies the biblical truth that we are blessed to bless others.

However, Somi's story isn't over. As I wrote earlier, she has recently got married. Despite all the tragedy she had already told me about, it was while she recounted this part of her story that she burst into floods of tears.

She met her new husband just before the Covid lockdown when he was labouring outside the gates to Mahima Griha, helping to install new water pipes. He already has a son from a previous marriage who lives with him since his wife ran off. During the lockdown, he and Somi spoke regularly on the phone and began to fall in love. He told her that he was divorced, and she was aware that he wasn't a Christian. Their wedding took place in her village; however, none of his family was present. She told me it was just a simple ceremony as neither of them were virgins. They prayed and exchanged *khadas*, the traditional Nepali scarves.

Somi's son has no paperwork, and her new husband promised to provide all this if she married him. She was also encouraged into this dubious marriage by local bureaucrats. I am particularly angered by the advice she was given at her local Village Development Committee (VDCs are Nepal's lowest form of administrative unit, which despite the name, cover all areas of Nepal, including towns and cities) where she had applied for a birth certificate for her son. Though women are legally entitled to make the application, the chauvinistic officials told her to get married so that a man could sort all the paperwork out for her. A birth certificate and citizenship are necessary for education, employment, travel and land ownership; without them, her son would almost certainly struggle through his life.

Since their marriage, her husband has come good on his promise to obtain documentation for her son, but there is a huge problem. He has named himself the father, which Somi was prepared to accept, but devastatingly he has named his first wife as the mother. It turns out they were not divorced, and now Somi has lost all legal rights to her son. She is also in danger of being prosecuted for polygamy if the authorities find out about their recent marriage.

It is unclear whether Somi's husband's intentions are nefarious. Sons are highly prized in traditional Nepali culture, and WWR helps other women who have lost access to their sons due to cruel in-laws. There is also a considerable market for trafficked children. Does he have any of these schemes in mind, or does he believe he was being helpful by obtaining a birth certificate, even if it contains the wrong names? Worryingly, her husband refuses to take Somi to meet his family and seems to be enjoying torturing his first wife by declining to divorce her.

As for me, I can't believe that a man has the power to deny a mother legal access to her child while simultaneously making another woman legally responsible without her permission either. WWR is in the process of engaging a lawyer to help, and on International Women's Day 2021, we invited an advocate from the Legal Aid and Consultancy Centre to meet with Somi (and several of our other women) to give advice. It has also occurred to me that a DNA test might prove helpful evidence that they are mother and son, but the cost is prohibitive. We have assured Somi that we will support her and, if required, will fight for her son to remain with her, but she remains ill at ease. I pray that God would speak to her, as he did before when she came so close to ending her life, and that she would be assured of his love and care for her. He has brought her so far; I know he won't abandon her now.

4

Warrior: Kopisha

To celebrate International Women's Day in March 2021, Esther and Nina had invited a women's advocate from the Legal Aid and Consultancy Centre (LACC) to spend the morning giving counsel at WWR's residential women's home, Mahima Griha. We had encouraged several of our women with ongoing legal issues to share their stories with her. Together we sat in Mahima Griha's main meeting room, and the women took turns to share their heartbreaking tales as she patiently listened and then offered her advice. I did my best to understand their Nepali, but it was beyond me most of the time. Thankfully, I had engaged the help of a new translator called Saru; it was unfair of me to keep relying on Esther when she was busy organizing the day's events. Saru is a charming pastor's wife whose wider family had shunned her when her father contracted leprosy. She was hugely sympathetic to the situations our women found themselves in.

Around ten women recounted how they had suffered from legal discrimination due to either lack of citizenship, bigamy, ostracism from in-laws or inheritance disputes. There were many tears, not only from those who addressed the room but from those listening who sympathized with their anguish. Among the women who spoke that day was Kopisha, for whom there had been many instances of suffering in her life.

In particular, she had suffered during the Maoist uprising. I was keen to include her story in this book as the Maoists have made an enormous impact on life in Nepal, and it is impossible to understand the current situation in the country without knowing the history of the Maoists.

Just a few days later, I arranged to go to Kopisha's house. This trip was a little different from my previous interviews with women. First off, the British Army had eased up on its Covid travel restrictions. Though still unable to use public taxis, I was allowed to pre-book a private hire vehicle to take us to her house. It felt good to leave the area around my house and see more of Kathmandu. Secondly, for this visit, Saru accompanied me to help and interpret, and I was happy to spend more time with her.

Saru and I met outside Ekta Books, a long-standing landmark in Patan and midway between our houses. It was one of the first publishers and booksellers in the country and is owned by a Christian family. Esther had told me that the family is the wealthiest Christian family in Nepal. The shop itself looks rather unremarkable from the street. Inside there used to be a rabbit warren of rooms, and books filled every space, as the shop stretched up several floors. Nowadays, the shop only occupies the ground floor. However, there are still the latest bestselling books from the West alongside obscure titles that are only available in Nepal. Thanks to Kathmandu's dusty atmosphere, it is hard to keep anything clean in the city, so an army of cleaners is employed to dust and tidy the shelves.

Saru and I set off in the private hire car and soon discovered the driver was quite a maniac. We tore along the ring road on the wrong side of the road and turned towards the city's Pepsicola area, named for a large bottling plant. Kathmandu always seems crowded, but it feels as if there are more shops than people in this area. The stores all seem to sell the same things, though, so I have no idea how they each stay in business. I did notice the Rhubarb Pharmacy; there are many shops in Kathmandu with English names, and I often wonder how their Nepali owners choose what to call them. Do they stick a pin in a dictionary, or was there some logic behind their choice of Rhubarb?

As we neared Bhaktapur, the streets opened up, and it was possible to catch glimpses of open fields. Women appeared trudging along with *dokos* (traditional woven baskets) on their backs full of bright red chilli peppers. We were due to meet Kopisha at Amar Singh *chowk*, a five-way intersection, and we stopped periodically to ask passers-by where it was. Even with my limited Nepali, I could understand that it was a short distance away. Still, our impetuous driver headed off in a different direction, and we then had to spend a quarter of an hour retracing our steps. Eventually, we spotted Kopisha, and I prepared to get out of the car; instead, she jumped in, and we headed off again. With Kopisha to direct us, there was no possibility of getting lost. We were soon at her bright and spotlessly clean home, which took up the ground floor of a concrete building. She served us a fluorescent green fizzy drink, put her yapping dog outside, and we began to talk.

Kopisha was born in Nepal's mid-west region in a village called Bada Bhairab; she is a direct descendant of a tribal king and is considered high-born. I've since looked up her village on Google Maps, and it appears to be incredibly remote. It is just a small collection of houses perched along a narrow path on a ridge. The track zigzags back and forth, indicating inhospitable and steep terrain. Though I'd love to visit, it doesn't look very accessible.

Born in the Nepali year 2027 (1970), Kopisha was the second of six children and had two sisters. The family was Hindu and performed *puja* every day. *Puja* is translated as worship and is usually practised every day by Hindus in their own homes. Each member of the household bows to idols, which are set up in small shrines in the corner of rooms, and offers food and flowers to their gods. In our first military quarter in Kathmandu, which was rented from a wealthy Sherpa guide, there was a locked *puja* room on the top floor. I felt uncomfortable knowing we were living in a house containing a room full of idols, but took heart that our God is mightier.

Kopisha wasn't keen on taking part in *puja* and could miss it when she wanted to. Girls from high-status families are often more subjugated than other women since their families cling tightly to the perception that they are 'pure' or 'unpolluted'. Yet, in Kopisha's case, her father was progressive, and since he was a village headman with influence, he permitted her to attend school. She and her sisters were the only girls who went to the small village primary school, which she attended from age 6 until 12. Despite her father's liberal outlook, some Brahmin traditions continued, though. Once her period began, she was subjected to the ordeal of *chhaupadi*; she spent those days in the cowshed.

On Saturdays, the only day off during Nepal's week, she and her family walked to their nearest bazaar in Dailekh to buy goods they could not produce for themselves, such as salt and fertilizer. She told me it was a four-hour journey each way and threw her hand in the air to demonstrate the steep topography; two hours up, two hours down and two river crossings. Again, a quick scour on Google Maps added detail to her description; the walk looked perilous through both jungle and deep valleys. The journey home must have been even more arduous as everything the family bought had to be carried home on their backs.

When just 14 years old, Kopisha's uncle suggested that she spend a few weeks in Dailekh to receive training about running a health post. The idea was that she would help out at the health post in Bada Bhairab. It was while staying in Dailekh that she encountered Christians for the first time. There was a church in Dailekh led by Brahman believers, yet attended by people from all castes. She heard children singing songs at the Sunday school, and then a miracle occurred. A low-caste Dalit man, who was well-known to her since he ploughed her family's fields, went along to the church and was healed of his mental illness. For the next twenty years, this man continued to work for her family, so she knows that his healing was long-lasting and genuine. He is now a pastor. Kopisha did not convert to Christianity at this point; however, the church and the Christians she met made an enduring and favourable impression on her.

Most of the men in Kopisha's extended family worked either for the police or the Royal Nepalese Army. Her family took pride in their patriotism, and they were well-connected and influential. Her father was of such importance that he had police guards assigned to him. One of these guards took a liking to Kopisha, and together with her elder brother and uncle, he conspired to marry her. While Kopisha was at her uncle's house in Dailekh, this man abducted her and forced her to marry him. She had no idea she was about to be carried off, and her brother and uncle allowed him to do so, thinking it was a good match. Her brother even wrote her a letter telling her that he would disown her if she didn't go through with the marriage. Sadly, the chauvinistic way this man handled Kopisha was to characterize the next few years of Kopisha's life. It was a clear indicator of how he had been raised to treat women. Kopisha would no longer enjoy the protection of her progressive father; the contrast between her old and new life was extreme.

Once the two of them were married, they moved into rented police accommodation in another district, away from both their families. She told me that the lodgings weren't too bad. Despite their bad start, her new husband behaved well, perhaps motivated by a desire to do his duty to keep up the appearance of a respectable marriage. Eventually, his father, a high-caste Hindu priest and shaman, heard about their union and came to fetch them back to his home in Humla, a high-altitude district in Nepal's far-west region. He was delighted that his son had married a direct descendant of the Dailekh tribal king and organized a marriage celebration for them.

By now, Kopisha was pregnant, yet the police force assigned her husband to Nepalgunj in Nepal's hot and humid Terai. Though also in the west of Nepal, the city is at a low altitude and has an entirely different climate. Kopisha remained with her in-laws in their home as tradition dictates; she belonged to them now. Since her father-in-law was a priest and healer, there was a lot of idol worship, and she had to perform *puja*. Similarly, they were strict about *chhaupadi*. When the time came to give birth, she delivered her daughter, with minimum assistance, in the cowshed. Following the birth, she had to remain there for several days until custom decreed her ritually pure again.

The concept of purity and remaining unpolluted is both a lifelong and daily obsession for many high-caste Nepali families. In her book *While the Gods Were Sleeping*, American anthropologist Elizabeth Enslin describes her experience of living with high-caste in-laws, having met and married a Nepali student at university. She was not allowed to do any cooking since she was considered impure. When she once turned down the stove because the food was burning, the family threw the entire meal away. She also gave birth while living with them and describes the birthing rituals in some detail. Her book is not for the fainthearted, and I don't recommend reading it if you are pregnant, but her perspective is unique.

Since Kopisha had given birth to a girl, her husband didn't bother leaving his police post to come home to see her or the baby. Her in-laws repeatedly told her that it would have been better if her daughter hadn't been born. These weren't just empty words; Kopisha was treated with contempt by them because she had given birth to a girl. They put her to work in the fields from dawn till dusk and kept her from her daughter. Meanwhile, they neglected to feed their granddaughter, and before she was 18 months old, she had died from their mistreatment.

Each of us was in floods of tears as Kopisha related this part of her story. I found the barbarity of it hard to comprehend; how could anyone do this to a young child? Let alone grandparents to their grandchild. The immorality of their actions over a sustained period is incomprehensible. Kopisha's father-in-law was a Hindu priest and intent on remaining unpolluted, yet he oversaw the murder of his granddaughter. I felt a whirl of emotions as Kopisha shared with us; simultaneously I was furious, utterly bewildered and desperately sad. I know that her in-laws were products of their culture and religion, having been taught that girls were worthless from their childhoods. Yet when a culture perverts such basic human virtues, like caring for a baby, it is clear that evil has built a stronghold. Even Jesus, in Matthew 7:11, affirms that fathers know how to give good gifts to their children; it is a natural instinct. On the way home, I told Saru that the couple would end up in prison if this happened in the UK. She believes femicide still occurs now, and families continue to get away with it.

Kopisha's daughter's name was Pushpa. This is her real name, and I told Kopisha I would include her name in this book in memory of her.

Understandably, Kopisha was distraught at her daughter's death. Although adult Hindus are cremated when they die, the corpses of children are buried since their souls are not thought to have such an attachment to their physical bodies. The act of cremation is considered to free an adult soul from the body. Consequently, her daughter's body was buried in the jungle. Kopisha visited the grave and sobbed uncontrollably over it. An elderly woman appeared who comforted her but took her back to her cruel mother-in-law, who told her that it would have been better if Kopisha had died as well.

One of the very few benefits of *chhaupadi* is that it allows women who are abused by their families to escape their oppression for a few days each month. The brief interlude, without constant harassment, gives the women space to heal both mentally and physically. If their periods coincide, women can talk to each other without the other household members overhearing. A few days after Kopisha first visited the grave, both she and her teenage sister-in-law were in the cowshed together for *chhaupadi*. Kopisha crept out at night with a rope; she intended to end her life by hanging herself over the grave of her daughter. Thankfully, her young sister-in-law heard her leave and sneaked along behind her through the forest. Just as Kopisha was about to put the rope around her neck, her sister-in-law intervened to stop her. As they walked back to their home and the cowshed, her sister-in-law revealed that she also loathed her parents for what they had done to Pushpa. She promised to support Kopisha as much as she could, and after that, she smuggled food to her and helped her with the never-ending household chores.

The two women also managed to communicate with Kopisha's husband. They stressed to him that Kopisha could not continue living with her in-laws since life with them was utterly intolerable. Consequently, a couple of years later, when the police reassigned her husband to Mugu, Kopisha went to live with him. Nepalis consider Mugu to be near Humla as it is just a few days' walk between the two; though they are adjacent districts, to travel between them means crossing a high mountain ridge covered in snow. It was while living there that Kopisha became pregnant once more and gave birth to a son. She delivered him in a cowshed again, but this time their landlord's kindly wife did as much as she could to help.

Just a few months later, they were on the move again and returned to her husband's previous posting in Nepalganj. Hearing all about these house moves, I wished I could talk to Kopisha without an interpreter's help; I felt we had a lot in common. I told her that my husband also got moved about with the British Army. She smiled; I'm confident we could be close friends if the circumstances were different. I also got the impression that despite the aggressive start to their marriage, when her husband abducted her, Kopisha believes that he was a good man. Perhaps once away from his parents' influence, he was able to care for her. Again, this was impressed upon me when Kopisha told me that her husband did not force her to attend her mother-in-law's funeral.

Kopisha was pregnant for the third time, and the police force selected her husband for a post in Jumla. To make life easier for Kopisha, they felt it best for her to return to her maternal home for the delivery. Returning home, even for a good reason, can be considered shameful in Nepal. Tradition dictates that once a woman marries into her husband's family, 'she must die there'. However, her husband respectfully asked her brother to take care of her, and she returned without shame. Kopisha laughed as she related that once again, she gave birth in a cowshed. Eleven days later, her husband appeared in time for the traditional baby-naming ceremony. On this day, the mother is declared ritually clean and can leave the cowshed to return to live with the rest of the household.

There may have been other reasons for placing Kopisha and their two sons with her maternal family. In the mid to late 1990s, the Maoists were active in the west of Nepal, and it would have been safer for them to live in a remote village rather than near a police post.

Democracy in Nepal is very new and remains fragile. For more than two hundred years, high caste kings and Rana prime ministers ruled the country from Kathmandu. They had little interest in furthering their citizens' prospects, and the country remained closed off from the rest of the world until the 1950s. These rulers even banned schools and foreign technology; their leaders didn't want the people to get above themselves.

During the twentieth century, calls for democracy became increasingly loud. From the 1930s, political parties began to organize on the fringes of Nepali society. Though they were banned, they attracted a following as the population realized how downtrodden they were. In 1951, the parties conspired with the beleaguered King Tribhuvan to create a new government, and held elections. However, this experiment with democracy was short-lived. King Tribhuvan died in 1955, and his progressive ideas were lost with him. His son, King Mahendra, took over and in 1960 banned political parties, imprisoned their leaders and introduced the *Panchayat* system. *Panch* is the Nepali word for five, and *Panchayat* means an assembly of five.

The *Panchayat* system gave all executive powers to the king, and he became a kind of dictator. Officials were elected to represent the people at village, town, district and national level, but only those favoured by the king had any chance of getting on the ballot. Their loyalty to the king was closely monitored, and they would find themselves banished from politics if they defied him. However, the political parties did not disappear and continued to organize underground. Governments of other nations supported their calls for democracy and, having observed the end of the USSR and the falling of the Berlin wall in 1989, they were inspired to act. In 1990 the parties called on their supporters to take to the streets in the first *Jana Andolan*, or people's uprising. They called on King Birendra, who had succeeded Mahendra, to reinstate multi-party democracy. After two months, in which it is thought 200,000 people marched and dozens of people were killed, the king bowed to the pressure and agreed to meet their demands.

Not everyone was satisfied with this new state of affairs. Left-wing and communist parties felt incredibly disappointed and did not think the king had gone far enough. King Birendra still retained a substantial amount of executive power and, in particular, had sole control of the Royal Nepalese Army. Besides, the new government system was not functioning well; between 1990 and 1994, eight unstable coalition governments fought among themselves, doing little to help the country develop. Nepal and its people remained desperately poor while its leaders enriched themselves.

Tired of the political wrangling, a charismatic leader named Prachanda came to the fore. In 1996, Prachanda and his comrades decided it was time to act and formed the Communist Party of Nepal (Maoist). They submitted a forty-point list of demands to the prime minister, the central two being a call for revolutionary land reform and the Hindu monarchy's end. These mandates were popular among the nation's marginalized rural underclass, and party ranks swelled. When the party voted for armed revolt, both men and women were prepared to fight with them. Henceforth, a period of bloody violence began that would continue for the next decade.

Known as the People's War, the Maoists began fighting with just two rifles. Having received some training from retired

Indian Gorkha soldiers,[4] they started their campaign in the west of Nepal. Using guerrilla tactics, they attacked police posts and acquired more weapons each time they did so. Prachanda was a master tactician, and even though he was constantly on the move to avoid arrest, he oversaw a growing insurgency. At its peak, the conflict involved 30,000 fighters and caused the death of 13,000 Nepali citizens; many more remain unaccounted for.

Both Kopisha and her husband were living in areas where the Maoists were highly active. In 1999, the Maoists launched an attack on the police post in Jumla, where her husband was stationed. Thirty-five policemen were killed in the skirmish, and her husband was only able to escape because he feigned his own death. He lay on the ground and pretended that he had been shot. One of Kopisha's uncles was also there and was killed. When it was safe to do so, her husband bolted from the compound and eventually made his way to Kathmandu.

While most of the country was enduring violence and undergoing radical change at the Maoists' hands, Kathmandu remained somewhat oblivious to what was going on. If an incident didn't occur within the capital's ring road, people joked that the government was utterly clueless. For example, when we lived there in 2005, towards the end of the People's War, the Maoists planted a bomb outside a rural school. They set a timer for it to go off at the end of the school day when the children departed for home. Thankfully the bomb went off early, and no one was harmed. Even though it was unsuccessful, I'm sure that if an attempt on children's lives had occurred anywhere in the West, it would have made global headlines. In one of Kathmandu's daily newspapers, though, it only featured on page three. There was such little interest in the Maoists' actions and a lack of concern for rural youngsters.

For Kopisha's husband, however, Kathmandu represented safety and a chance to gain some respite from his constant fear of the Maoists. Once there, he resigned from the police and set himself up as a herbal trader. His new business required him to travel back to his remote home district, which the Maoists controlled, to collect herbs. On several occasions, they accosted him and made him pay bribes. I asked Kopisha if he experienced any post-traumatic stress disorder, and she nods enthusiastically. Yes, he was traumatized, she told me.

Meanwhile, Kopisha was back in her maternal home and also having to cope with the Maoists' brutal arrival. Since the men in her family were well-connected to the police and army, one by one, they moved into army and police barracks where they thought they would be safer. Not all of them survived. Eventually, only Kopisha, her two young sons and her elderly grandmother remained at their home. However, a detachment of Maoist fighters soon joined them, who took over their property and turned it into a barracks. The soldiers forced them to provide board and lodging for more than a year. When the Maoists discovered that Kopisha was married to a policeman, they attempted to shoot her. Thankfully the bullet missed her, but it hit and killed an ox instead.

Sadly, while in Kathmandu, her husband 'married' another woman. I wonder if this was because, thanks to his chauvinistic upbringing, he was incapable of looking after himself. Perhaps a new wife was just a convenience, someone to cook and clean. One way or another, news reached him of Kopisha's situation. He returned to Bada Bhairab to collect her and his two children and brought them safely to Kathmandu. I could tell that, although hurt at the news of his new marriage, Kopisha was hugely grateful for his actions. Regrettably, her grandmother was left behind, and she passed away a year later.

Once safely in Kathmandu, Kopisha told me her 'normal life' began. Her husband abandoned her, but I sensed she was relieved to finally have a chance to live on her own without scrutiny from other family members. Life was not easy, but at least she was free to make decisions for herself. Like so many impoverished women, she found work as a labourer. She worked in the same fields I had spotted on the way to her home, carrying sand to and from the riverbank and filtering it. It was incredibly arduous work.

One day, a man and some well-behaved children, clearly not all his own, came to fetch filtered sand. They only needed two sacks of it, a relatively small quantity, so Kopisha let them take it for free. Moved at her generosity, the man asked if she was a Christian believer. It turned out that the man was a pastor, and together with children from the Christian hostel he ran, they were building a church, hence the need for sand. The driver of their vehicle invited Kopisha to church the following Saturday, and she eagerly accepted the invitation. After marriage, her life had been one of seclusion within the family, and her in-laws and husband rigorously controlled who she met with. This was the first opportunity since her childhood, when she witnessed the Dalit man's miraculous healing in her home town, to investigate Christianity.

The following Saturday, she and her younger son took two buses to Gwarko to attend the Anantashalom (Eternal Peace) Church. She was impressed by the kindness of everyone and felt happy to be there. She has been attending the same church each week ever since. In the beginning, there were around thirty-five attendees, but it now has 200 members. On her third week, the pastor's wife took her aside and they had a long conversation about everything that had happened to Kopisha in her life. Kopisha felt as if this woman was her guardian and called her Guruama (teacher-mother). At the end of their conversation, Guruama asked if Kopisha wanted to accept Jesus, but Kopisha said she didn't know how to. After a full explanation, they prayed together, and Kopisha became a Christian.

Another five years passed, during which time Kopisha learnt more about Christianity and became confident in her faith. The Maoist uprising also ended, and a peace agreement was signed in 2006 that dismissed the Hindu monarchy. In 2001 the crown prince had opened fire on the king and eight other royal family members before turning the gun on himself. Though the king's brother Gyanendra took over as king, the entire royal family's legitimacy was in doubt. If they were supposed to be incarnations of Hindu gods, why had this tragedy befallen them? Coupled with the Maoists' calls for reform, change in Nepal became inevitable. The country slowly transitioned from a Hindu kingdom to a secular republic. As part of the peace agreement, the Maoists laid down their arms, meaning it was now safe for Kopisha to return to her home village.

The family planned a reunion over *Dashain*; Kopisha's younger brother would also return from Dubai, where he was a migrant worker, to join them. As a Christian, Kopisha did not want to accept the Hindu *tika* blessings from her family members, so she snuck off to tend goats on a distant hillside when they were due to perform this rite. When she returned to the house after dark, her parents asked why she had not been present earlier, and she revealed that she had become a Christian. Their immediate reaction was to accuse her of polluting them, and they called her a beef-eater. The cow is a sacred animal in Hinduism, and in Nepal, the punishment for killing one is twelve years in prison. They threw her and her son out of the house and destroyed the pots and water she had touched. Given that Kopisha was related to most residents of the village, everyone soon heard about her conversion. She was pursued out of the community and ended up sleeping outdoors at a school that night. In the morning, she telephoned Guruama, who offered comfort and encouraged her to return to Kathmandu.

Though committed to her faith, Kopisha had not felt confident of getting baptized before this incident. Now, she had nothing to lose, and so once back in Kathmandu, she was baptized with twelve other church members in the Godavri River. There was a party and dancing afterwards, and she felt the Holy Spirit.

In her view, life is getting easier and easier for Christians in Nepal; they are now regarded positively by broader society. She told me of a recent incident: the police arrested three men for drug use and disorderly behaviour. Though not Christian themselves, the police instructed the men to start attending church to straighten themselves out. It seems the police are now missionaries.

In the recent past, landlords would not let out rooms to Christians for fear of pollution. Nowadays, landlords are keen to rent rooms to Christians who are considered well-behaved and good tenants. Kopisha's own landlord and neighbours repeatedly ask her to pray for them, although they are Hindu.

As for her future, she longs to return to her home district and preach the gospel there. To do this, she believes she needs more schooling and training in theology. Unfortunately, the church is unable to support her as a missionary, and she can't afford time off from work to study. Promisingly, her family is now eager to hear the gospel. Having witnessed the struggles in her life, how she has overcome them and can forgive, they want to know how it is possible. They marvel at her lack of bitterness, and I do too. I have described her as a warrior in the chapter title because she has always persevered and takes on every challenge with faith and expectation. Having bravely endured the Maoist occupation of her home, it seemed an apt description for her. I hope and pray she can fulfil her dreams of being an evangelist in Nepal's remote and mountainous districts. The words of Isaiah 40:9–11 are my prayer for her; may she climb mountains and preach the good news.

5

Friend: Suki

At the end of March 2021, a grey pall came over the Kathmandu sky. The sun burned orange above us all day, and from late afternoon onwards, it shone red. The post-apocalyptic atmosphere resulted from farmers in Nepal and North India burning stubble to prepare their fields for planting the next crop. Countless forest fires across the country also added to the smog. It hadn't rained for months.

On many days in April, Kathmandu topped the leaderboard for the most polluted city in the world, an accolade no nation wants to win. In response, the government closed schools for a week, meaning that children didn't have to journey to school while their eyes and throats stung. The closures also prevented beaten-up school buses from churning out more pollution. Kathmandu airport closed for several days as visibility was so poor, and while indoors, my family and I had to turn on the lights. For the women that WWR supports, however, electricity is a much more expensive commodity. They moved around in the dim light and learnt to cope with the decreased visibility. Each of us stayed inside as much as we could, and all of us longed for blue skies.

Eventually, following several days of dramatic thunderstorms, the skies cleared. Once again, we could see the hills surrounding the Kathmandu Valley and no longer felt trapped in smog and cloud. As I walked the short journey with Saru from my house to Suki's room, I marvelled at the green hills. I could identify buildings clinging to the steep sides that I hadn't seen since my return to Nepal. It was stunningly beautiful. The air smelt and tasted so good.

The two of us met Suki across the ring road, near a driving test centre where the test-takers drive around cones to prove they are worthy of a licence. There is no need for them to demonstrate road safety or an ability to cope with traffic, which does explain a lot about the reckless driving habits of Nepal's motorists. The offices of small car insurance brokers lined the streets, presumably so that car insurance can be arranged immediately once a driving licence has been granted. On this particular day, it seemed the brokers weren't paying out, and clients were shouting and arguing with the agents inside. I thought a fight might break out at any moment.

Standing in front of a newly built small Hindu temple, we waited for Suki to arrive. I had met her many times before, as WWR has supported her for a long while, but she always wears a shawl wrapped tightly around her head, making it hard to recognize her. Traditionally Nepali women wear *kurtas*, consisting of three parts: a long top, loose pyjama bottoms and a shawl or scarf. The three pieces are bought as a set, and the fabric of each part matches the others. Since it is usually hot in Kathmandu, the thin scarves are normally draped loosely over women's shoulders but, unusually, Suki wraps hers around her head. The reason she wore it this way is a key part of her story. Once I had identified her, we hugged and began following her to her room along newly paved, wide roads.

Outside Suki's house were magnificent rose bushes that her landlord had planted. There was also a vast collection of flip-flops on the ground. It's customary in Nepal to take off your shoes before entering a house, and we added ours to the colourful assortment. Despite consisting of just a few floors and rooms, it was clear from the number of shoes that many people lived in the property. The landlord evidently looked after the house well, making it a popular place to stay. Suki's room was exceptionally bright and clean; even the front of her fridge was still wrapped in the clear plastic it arrived in, although it was no longer new. As she didn't have a bed, she invited us to sit on her mattress on the floor. Suki found herself a stool – it couldn't have been more than 4ins high – and before perching on it to tell us her story, she made us cups of sweet tea.

Now around 60 years old, Suki was born in Kavre district, the area adjacent to Kathmandu on its eastern border. She has an older brother, two younger sisters, and her father was a soldier in the Royal Nepalese Army. He would return home very infrequently, spending years at a time stationed in Nepal's Terai. Consequently, all the responsibility for childrearing fell on Suki's mother and grandmother, who lived with them. Her mother received very little financial support from her husband, so she and his mother were forced to work long hours for local landowners in their fields. The family lived in a single room, and an open fire in the middle of it was their only means of cooking and keeping warm.

One day, when her mother was out collecting water and Suki was just 5 months old, Suki rolled off their bed and into the fire. She has no idea how long she was in the fire, but by the time her mother found her, she was close to death. Frantically, her mother tipped the water she had just retrieved on the fire to put it out and scooped up Suki. Then, in a great example of community cooperation, the men in her village took turns to carry Suki in a *doko* to Bir Hospital in Kathmandu. The journey would have taken about three hours, and I can only assume Suki's mother hurried along with them.

Once in hospital, Suki received treatment for the severe burns she had endured and spent three months in the ward, recovering. Having no money to pay for her care, her mother took a loan to cover the costs. To this day, Suki's neck and torso are covered in scars. The skin is in parts stretched tautly, wrinkled or discoloured. The wounds are upsetting and difficult to look at and are why she still wraps a shawl so tightly around her head. For the first time since we arrived, she revealed her neck, decolletage and waist to Saru, who had not met her before. The distorted skin looked painful even though the accident took place so many decades ago, and we asked her if it hurts. She told us she feels a lot of pain in the areas where the skin is stretched tight, although the scars didn't cause her any pain when she was younger.

Suki's parents did not allow her to go to school. Instead, she stayed at home to look after her younger sisters and the family's livestock while her mother and grandmother were labouring. However, her older brother was permitted to go to school. He attended the village primary along with all the other local boys. There was no secondary provision, and no girls received an education in their area.

While at home, one of her tasks was to clean the *pujako thali*, a plate (*thali*) with multiple sections used in Hindu worship (*puja*). Her family attended the *mandir* (local temple) every day to present offerings and had to do so with empty stomachs. Suki doesn't know why they had to fast each day and did not believe in the Hindu deities they worshipped but went along with the family ritual.

Despite preparing most of the household meals, Suki's mother did not want her to sit with the rest of the family at mealtimes. Tragically, Suki's skin had not healed correctly following her burns, and her chin was now permanently stuck to her chest. Eating and drinking were tricky and messy. Food dribbled out of her mouth, and her family did not want to look at her as she struggled to feed herself. Sometimes they beat her, and they forced her to eat alone in the corner of the room.

Sadly, this situation occurs frequently in Nepal, and Naomi Reed describes several instances in her book *My Seventh Monsoon*.[5] Naomi and her husband were both missionary physiotherapists. They served for several years in Pokhara, where Eileen Lodge first set up a hospital. Naomi describes how, for many Nepalis, seeking treatment following a burn injury is usually left far too late. A trip to the hospital could involve many days of walking and meant time away from tending their land. Consequently, by the time they arrived, the skin of the burnt limb, which is usually most comfortable flexed, had fused with any adjoining skin. She saw calves stuck to thighs and arms adhered to torsos. Although Suki had spent three months in hospital, since she was only a baby when she returned home, I doubt she would have been strong enough to hold up her head. Her chin had fallen against her chest and remained there.

When Suki was 10, her younger sisters were considered old enough to look after themselves, so Suki joined her mother and grandmother in the fields. Although she was working tirelessly for her family, the abuse from them and some of their neighbours became worse. They called her a devil and labelled her a burden since they assumed no one would want to marry her. To her face, they told her it would be better for her to die. They justified their abuse of her by appealing to karma. The prevailing Hindu attitude in Nepal is that one gets what one deserves; in their eyes, Suki must have performed some evil act for her injuries to have occurred. To them, it was her fate to roll into the fire as a baby. The gods must have caused it because she deserved it, and they would do well to keep away from such a wretched girl.

Eventually, sometime before the age of 15, though Suki isn't exactly sure when, her mother physically threw her out of the house. I asked Suki if her mother drank alcohol and if her rage could be put down to intoxication. Suki assured me her mother didn't drink; sadly, she completely rejected Suki knowing exactly what she was doing.

Thankfully, Suki had friends in her village, and one of them took her in. Suki described this girl as worldly; her father was a *Thulo Manche* which literally means 'big man' but is better translated as 'important man' or perhaps 'big wig'. This girl frequently travelled with her father to Kathmandu and knew the hospitals there. Regrettably, Suki wanted to die by now, but she decided that the best place to die was in a hospital. Presumably not knowing Suki's decision, her friend took her to Shanta Bhawan, the missionary hospital that had also helped Lila. Thankfully, Suki did not die; instead, the hospital performed an operation to separate her chin from her chest and allowed her to spend six months recovering.

When Suki returned to her family and village, they were not pleased to see her. They told her that they did not care if she was dead or alive, and they had not searched for her. A rumour had reached them that Suki was in the hospital, but they hadn't bothered to confirm it. They packed her off to her aunt's house, whom she called Thulo Ama (older-mother), one day's walk away.

When Suki was 20 years old, her period began. Starting menstruation this late is unusual but may have been caused by malnutrition; it is difficult to determine what caused the delay so many years later. The village she lived in did not require her to live in a *chhaupadi* hut for the days of her period. Yet, she was obliged to go to a neighbour's house so that men could not see her and she could not see the sun. Even now, she doesn't complain about having had to do this; perhaps spending time with her neighbours was pleasant for her and a welcome break from her household chores.

The start of her period meant that Suki, according to the traditions of her tribe and caste, was now considered old enough to marry. Unlike the Brahmin castes that insist on extreme purity, hence marriage before menstruation, she hails from a middle caste, so her marriage could wait until her period had begun. Her Thulo Ama took it upon herself to arrange the marriage, and Suki was surprised to discover that a good-looking 25-year-old man with no disabilities was interested in her. In fact, he approached her aunt rather than the other way round. At first, Suki refused him because he was a known drunk and had a reputation for sleeping around. However, her aunt persuaded her that he was the best and only offer she would get and that she should marry him. Sadly, it is unthinkable in Nepali culture for women to remain unmarried, and legally they remain vulnerable without a husband to represent them. The two of them had a small Hindu wedding in the presence of just a priest; neither of their families bothered to attend.

As soon as they were married and Suki had moved into the family home with his parents, he began to beat her. On one occasion, he severely battered her. Once again, her friends came to the rescue and took her to the local health post to have her head stitched up. Her husband had five brothers, and all of them and their wives despised her. At the time, her scars were very bright, and so they ridiculed and beat her. They included her husband in their derision and asked him why he had brought someone so deformed, weak and ugly into their home. Suki had to wake up early every day and carry out a never-ending series of chores.

In time, her husband began to ignore her entirely. He continued to drink and cheat on her. Their only contact was when he would turn up at their home to rape her. Thankfully, marital rape was declared a crime in Nepal in 2006, but this was long after Suki endured such intimate violence from her husband.

Just a year after their wedding, Suki gave birth to a daughter at home. Sadly, this was an opportunity for more discrimination. Usually, a new mother is offered regular meals containing meat after giving birth to regain her strength. She should also have benefited from another ritual whereby the women in the family massage the mother with oil to aid post-natal recovery. Suki was denied both of these; the birth of a daughter had further lowered her standing within the family. Even when she gave birth to three sons in quick succession afterwards, they were not enough to end her in-laws' loathing.

After enduring the wrath of her in-laws for so long, she was eventually kicked out by them. Suki was just 28, and her youngest son was only one or two months old. Bravely, she caught a bus to Kathmandu with her four children in tow and a single bag. A friend from her village had relocated to Kathmandu and returned each year for *Dashain*. Suki had the forethought to ask her where she lived, and so she headed there. The bus from her village took her to Ratna Park, an open area in the centre of Kathmandu. From there, she caught another bus to Lagankhel, the market area in Patan, one of the cities in the Kathmandu Valley. Once off the bus, she asked around until she found Ikhalakhu, a narrow and crowded street in the heart of Patan's old city. She stopped people in the street and asked for her friend by name; amazingly, she found her. Searching for her friend like this must have been like looking for a needle in a haystack. Given that she did all this with four tiny children hanging off her is incredible.

Typically, families in Kathmandu live in a single room, so Suki's friend could only put them up for one night. The following morning they sought out a nearby room for Suki to rent herself; thankfully, everything was cheaper in those days. She remembered that a bunch of spinach cost just 50 paisa (half a rupee, or less than half a pence), and room rent cost hundreds of rupees rather than the thousands it does today. Her friend also helped her find work as a labourer, and Suki was able to start immediately. I was upset to hear that she took her youngest two children with her to the worksites, and the older two were left locked inside their room. Life must have been unbearably difficult for her in those days. She told me that her husband would turn up from time to time to see his children, but he gave them nothing.

Already weakened by the fire incident and the regular beatings she had endured when living with her husband and in-laws, labouring made her sick regularly. A growth also developed on her neck, and she needed surgery. Mercifully, she had just enough money to afford the operation. Patan Hospital, a missionary hospital that originated from the groundwork laid by Shanta Bhawan Hospital, was nearby, and she was admitted there. At the time, United Mission to Nepal (UMN) oversaw the running of the hospital, and it was staffed by a mix of local and missionary doctors and specialists.

The greatest problem facing Suki was what to do with her children while she was in the hospital; the anticipated recovery period was around one month. I was speechless when she told me what she did with them; it would never have occurred to me and reflects the desperation and loneliness she must have felt at the time.

In Kathmandu there are many street children who roam about begging for food and money. Most of the children form gangs to give themselves some safety and a sense of community. On the day that Suki was due to have her operation, she took her children to one of these groups and left her children in their care. Although the children rove all over the city during the day, and it would be tricky to find them during daylight hours, she informed me that street children always sleep in the same location at night. After a month, sure enough, she found her children again and brought them home with her. She credits God with protecting her family.

It was while in Patan Hospital that Suki heard the gospel. A missionary called Jean visited the wards and told her about Jesus. Impressed by what she heard, Suki decided that *Isu Dharma* (Jesus truth) was good, and she prayed to accept him. Instantly she felt better both physically and mentally. Once out of the hospital, she bought a Bible for 20 rupees, although she couldn't read it. She carried it with her everywhere, and over a long period, she taught herself to read it; she is still learning today. Jean continued to visit her for several years afterwards and helped the family out with food and money.

One of the largest churches in Kathmandu is Koinonia Patan Church. Suki joined their women's fellowship, and after two or three years, she was baptized along with 150 others. Patan Church had a baptismal pool on the ground floor and space for everyone to enjoy a huge feast afterwards. She told me that dishes, including meat, were provided for them and it was a fabulous party. Nowadays, the church asks people to provide their own food for the celebration potluck, so Suki was glad that she was baptized before this rule was introduced.

During the following years, Suki's children also became Christians and were baptized. She informed her husband and in-laws about her new faith, but they didn't care since they already hated her.

In a practical sense, life was no easier for Suki, though. When returning from church one Thursday, having fasted all day, she knew there would be no food in the house when she got home. She decided to kill herself and threw herself down in the road in front of a jeep. Fortunately, she was seen and dragged out of the way before the jeep reached her. As she walked home, she spotted a shiny ten rupee coin on the ground. While stooping to pick it up, she noticed a bundle of notes containing 3,500 rupees. God had provided for her; the amount was enough to cover the cost of her children's school enrolment for the year.

It breaks my heart to write this, but the worst for Suki was yet to come. Since Suki laboured for long hours every day to scrape together enough to support her family, she relied on friends and neighbours to keep an eye on her children when they returned from school. By now, Suki's daughter was 12 or 13 and very beautiful; I have met her daughter and can vouch for this. A 20-year-old man from Suki's church helped out from time to time by watching the children. Though he claimed to be a Christian, gallingly, he was attracted to her daughter and began molesting her.

Both Suki and the church's leaders became aware of what was happening. They confronted the man, but his solution to the problem was to offer to marry Suki's daughter. Suki agreed to this arrangement; I'm sure she felt she had no choice, but it was a disastrous misjudgement. At the age of just 13, her daughter was married off and went to live with her abuser.

Shortly afterwards, this man told Suki's daughter to have sex with his boss even though both of them were respected civil servants. Suki doesn't know whether he forced her to go through with this or not, but word seems to have got out that a man was selling his pretty young wife for sex. A man from Balaju approached her daughter's husband and told him he could find a job for her. He offered to buy her, and her husband accepted the offer.

Just like that, Suki's daughter was sold, and she became a victim of human trafficking. Suki didn't see her again for ten years.

Some extraordinary books have been written by the victims of sex trafficking that detail what happened to them, the degradations they were forced to endure and their eventual escapes. I highly recommend *Radhika's Story* by Sharon Hendry, though it will sadden and enrage you. Yet, this is Suki's story; I want to focus on what it is like to be the mother of a trafficked girl before I reveal what happened to her daughter.

Suki told me she turned into a madwoman. She searched everywhere for her daughter, and when she confronted her daughter's husband, he told her that her daughter had run away. Suki didn't believe him but didn't know what to do. Going to the police seemed pointless. She felt as if she was going insane. Every night she prayed to God for her daughter and wept countless tears. She would often stay awake into the small hours praying and sobbing in the dark so that her sons wouldn't hear her distress.

Unbelievably, Suki told no one that her daughter had gone missing. Shame prevented her from doing so. She didn't tell her pastor, and her sons also didn't know what had happened. If her friends asked how her daughter was, she would not answer. Due to the clandestine nature of human trafficking, it is immensely challenging to gauge how many girls are trafficked from Nepal into India each year. Official estimates put the figure at between 5,000 and 15,000. With a 14-year-old daughter of my own, it distresses me to imagine all the mothers of these victims going silently crazy.

By now, WWR was supporting Suki to help with her rent and medical bills. She had not mentioned that she had a daughter to us. So it was with enormous surprise that in 2010, while I was visiting Kathmandu for two weeks, we heard that her daughter had turned up out of the blue.

During my time running WWR, meeting with Suki and her daughter that week was a seminal moment. As Esther and I met with the two of them, the room was filled with emotion. At times none of us could speak because we were unable to take in nor respond to all we were hearing. The weight of sorrow made it difficult to breathe.

Suki's daughter told us that she had gone to meet with the man from Balaju, and he had poisoned her. While unconscious, he had smuggled her over Nepal's open border with India. When she came to, she was well on her way to Delhi, where he sold her to a brothel. Over the next ten years, she was forced to have sex with around ten to twelve men each day. The brothel was like a prison, and she was physically abused if she did not comply. We saw the scars on her body from countless cigarette burns to prove it.

Surprisingly, Suki's daughter never became pregnant, even though the men who paid to have sex with her seldom used a condom, and she wasn't offered any contraceptives. However, she did witness the brothel owners carrying out brutal DIY abortions on the girls who were held captive with her. There were police raids too, but the brothel she worked in had secret doors at the back of cupboards that led to hiding places. She and the other women were made to cower in them and remain silent.

Yet, she did escape. Though I don't know for sure in Suki's daughter's case, from other literature I have read about sex-trafficking victims, as the girls grow older, they begin to have regular customers. Even though they are paying for sex, these men believe they are falling in love with the girls and can be manipulated to help them flee. By whatever means she managed to escape, I know that she worked as a labourer to buy her bus ticket home once she had got away from the brothel. Suki's daughter took several weeks to make the 500-mile journey from Delhi to Kathmandu.

When Esther and I met with Suki and her daughter in 2010, we had to do so in secret. During the ten years that her daughter had been in Delhi, Suki had moved rooms, so her daughter was compelled to ask her previous neighbours where her mum had gone. When she turned up, she looked and sounded different to how she was before. She spoke Hindi now, and even when speaking Nepali, she had an accent. She also looked exotic after years of having to apply heavy kohl make-up to her eyes. Regrettably, she could not return to her old life covertly, and all of Suki's neighbours were abuzz with the news that this girl had reappeared. Sadly, it was apparent to them that she had been a prostitute. Suki told me that in Kathmandu, if a single woman buys new clothes, her neighbours accuse her of being a prostitute because how else would she afford them? Her daughter's reappearance meant their neighbours were having a field day.

Such was the stigma surrounding her that even Suki's sons refused to speak to their sister. Suki and her daughter faced rejection again, and when we met them, they were trembling in their room. Yet despite the malicious gossip, Suki was absolutely delighted to see her daughter. She couldn't find the words to express both her astonishment that God had answered her prayers and horror at what her daughter had suffered.

When I left them that day, I was unable to stop thinking about everything that Suki's daughter had been through. Based on Psalm 23:5, 'You prepare a feast for me in the presence of my enemies. You honour me by anointing my head with oil. My cup overflows with blessings', God gave me a beautiful vision of him blessing Suki's daughter with an extravagant picnic on a beautiful mountainside. All those who had raped, abused and trafficked her were made to watch as Jesus honoured her. On the following Sunday, I was back at church in England, and by God-coincidence, the congregation sang 'The Lord is My Shepherd' based on Psalm 23 immediately before I was spontaneously asked to share about my trip to Nepal. The song meant so much to me, and I was in tears as I tried to explain what had happened to Suki. It was so difficult.

Back in Kathmandu and a few months after my visit, Suki managed to find a job for her daughter as a live-in cook. She still works there today, and the two of them speak to each other on the phone several times a day. Her daughter was due to come over a few hours after my visit to help Suki count her pills and take her medicine. Her daughter has some mental health problems due to the trauma she witnessed and because she was beaten over the head while at the brothel. However, it is clear that the two will look after each other from now on, and a unique bond holds them together. Their bond is also a commitment to keep silent about what happened in Delhi. Suki has never told anyone apart from Esther and me (and now Saru) about their ordeal; even her pastor remains in the dark. She still feels so much shame.

Appallingly, Suki's Christian sons still do not accept their sister. When they see their mother on the street, they do not acknowledge her either as they don't wish to be associated with someone so disfigured. Their attitudes deeply upset Suki, and I can't help feeling that if they showed their mother and sister some love and acceptance, many of the emotional wounds the two of them have suffered would be healed.

There is deep conflict within Suki. Though she loves God and is ever so grateful that her daughter returned to her, she questions why God allowed her to live when she rolled into the fire as a baby. She feels as if her life has been one long series of painful events and wonders if it might have been better if she had died then. Like the pollution I described above, her scars have cast a pall over every relationship in her life. She can't escape the aftermath of that incident though it was sixty years ago. My prayer for her is that the clouds would clear and her life would be filled with God's light and goodness.

Suki's ambition is to help others, and she is grateful to Jean, Eileen and WWR's staff, who have helped her over the years. If she can overcome her propensity to withdraw from people for fear of their rejection, she could be such an encouragement to them. She knows that God answers prayer and wants to inspire other people to keep on asking, even when it seems there is no hope. She has also had a dream that someone will buy her a small piece of land on which to build a house so her landlord and neighbours will stop mocking her. I'll leave that thought with you!

Listening to Suki and writing up her story has been the hardest to do so far. Although all the ladies I have written about have experienced great tragedy, Suki's story seems especially miserable. She wept continually through our conversation as there's been no let-up in the difficulties she's faced throughout her life. I wonder what my readers will make of such despair and how reading this will affect them? Thankfully, we have a God who can redeem everything and use it for his will. I entrust Suki's story to you and pray that rather than depressing you, he'll use it to achieve his good and perfect purposes.

6

Witness: Saru

In the days and weeks following my meeting with Suki, I felt as if my life entered a spin cycle. Everything happened so quickly it was hard to keep up, and I am writing this back in Wiltshire, England. Last week I interviewed Saru, my interpreter, from hotel quarantine in London.

Saru and I had interviewed Suki on a Thursday; by then, we were already aware of the enormous Covid resurgence in India. Daily reports from hospitals in India described wards full to bursting with Covid patients, and there was news of desperate oxygen shortages in India's capital. New Delhi is only 500 miles from Kathmandu, and there is an open border between Nepal and India. So, every resident of Kathmandu was on edge, waiting for the Covid tsunami to reach us and hoping that somehow Nepal would escape the worst.

On the Sunday following our interview, there were rumours that Nepal's government was about to announce another lockdown. They acted swiftly, and just the next day, we were informed that restrictions would begin in four days. Nepal's lockdowns are severe, and those intervening days were needed to stock up on supplies and prepare. Kathmandu's international airport, the only one in the country, would be closing, and shops would operate for minimal hours. Unlike the UK, exercise and walking would be prohibited; everyone was to remain in their homes, and police would be present on street corners across the city to enforce the rules. If the police caught someone out and about who shouldn't be, they made them stand in the street for an hour or two in stress positions.

Saru had been suffering from knee pain for several months. She wanted to fit in a visit to Patan Hospital for treatment before lockdown began, and so she attended the outpatients' clinic on the same Monday that lockdown was announced. On Tuesday, I met her outside Ekta Books again to hand over her pay. I wanted to ensure she had everything I owed her to help her gear up for and get through the lockdown. Together with her son and daughter, we walked towards a café for which she had a gift voucher. Everest Church, led by her husband, had encouraged its members to attend a marriage course at the café, and Saru had received the gift voucher as a thank you. She was heading there to treat her son and daughter to a meal before lockdown deprived them of the opportunity to go out and about. I walked with them for about ten minutes, wanting to grab a final conversation with Saru before I could no longer see her during the lockdown.

On Thursday, lockdown began. Initially, food shops were open from 5 a.m. till 10 a.m., then again from 5 p.m. until 7 p.m., but this was soon reduced to just two hours per day. The rules appeared counterintuitive, as the shops were bustling during these limited hours and seemed certain Covid hotspots. However, the rationale was that only those with a pass should be out and about when the shops were closed. Without such limited hours, it was thought that groups of young people would spend all day roaming the streets passing Covid between them. If the shops were open, it meant they could pretend they were on their way to buy groceries.

By the end of the first day of lockdown, my husband, Simon, was already conscious that all spouses and dependents at the British Camp might be evacuated back to the UK. For many, this would be their second evacuation, as just the previous year army dependents had been forced to leave when coronavirus was first identified (in fact, two wives had also been evacuated following the 2015 earthquake; for them, this would be their third evacuation). I had joined these families for ten weeks in the UK between leaving Alabama, where we had been previously posted by the army, before being allowed to fly to Nepal.

I settled into the lockdown rhythm, which meant getting up early to head to the shops to see what was available to buy before settling down for the rest of the day at home. I walked laps of the garden listening to podcasts in an attempt to maintain some level of fitness. Though life was quiet in a physical sense, since everyone was limited to their immediate vicinity, mentally, Simon and I felt as if we were running a marathon. News about the Covid situation poured in, and I barely saw Simon for the next month as he worked around the clock to determine if we should be evacuated and how.

Nepal had received some vaccines in March 2021 and had vaccinated most of the country's health workers and over-65s; there are very few of the latter. Then, various hospitals in Kathmandu Valley received batches of the vaccine on a mysterious rotating basis. If they could fathom the vaccine schedule, Nepalis went along to these hospitals early in the morning and queued up to receive their jabs. The same procedure for vaccine distribution was deployed in India, and it has subsequently been shown that the long chaotic lines for jabs caused the virus to spread.

In March, the Royal Air Force had flown out a batch of vaccines to the British Gurkhas in Nepal. All the army personnel had received their first vaccine. Yet, as the Covid wave swept into Kathmandu, the camp's civilian staff began to go down. So Simon took a potentially career-ending gamble and took the brave decision to give away our second doses to the local workforce. He had to go out on a limb since he didn't have official UK approval before instructing the camp's doctor to start putting our shots in local arms. However, it swiftly followed, which was a relief to all. I am very proud of him, and I am sure he prevented many of the British Army's local civilian staff from needing to be admitted to the hospital. He could even have saved lives.

Giving away our second jabs wasn't entirely altruistic, though, as it also benefited British Army personnel. With local staff vaccinated, it meant that we were inside a bigger 'bubble'. Additionally, we relied on these local employees to keep essential services such as drinking water and the camp's electricity supply going. So vaccinating them meant the risk to us from loss of vital services was significantly reduced.

Among the first pieces of news we received while confined to home was a rumour that the airport had been taken over by 'mafia' travel agents who saw the lockdown as an opportunity to make money. They arranged charter flights to fly people in and out of the country while charging double the usual ticket price. Allegedly, a government minister was in their pocket; it was said that they would continue to bribe him to keep the airport closed to regular carriers so their profits could be maximized. I had been expecting to fly home to see my children for the May half-term, but my flights were cancelled.

Missionary friends working at Patan Hospital, who had served in Nepal for decades, described one of their regular shifts on the Covid ward as their worst day ever. At one point, the hospital had only sixty minutes of oxygen remaining.

The stress of maintaining oxygen to patients took a massive toll on the staff. Each of them was jumpy as they repeatedly rushed to rescue their patients each time there was a hint that the oxygen was about to run out. On social media, posts advertising oxygen started popping up regularly; sometimes, a payment for the oxygen was required, at other times, oxygen was offered for free. Unfortunately, there was no quality control, and it was impossible to tell how reliable the oxygen on offer was.

More than one week after the start of lockdown, I heard the awful news that Saru was Covid-positive and in need of oxygen. Just the day after I had last seen her, a headache had begun. She had deteriorated slowly over the next week, adding new symptoms and ailments each day. By the time she took a PCR test, she was already severely weakened and suffering from a sore throat, fever and diarrhoea. For nine days, her temperature had not budged from 38.3C (101F). She believed she had picked up the virus while visiting the outpatients' department for her knee. So she had already contracted coronavirus when I last met her on the way to the café.

Saru's WhatsApp message to let me know she had Covid was brief, and it soon became apparent that she was too unwell to communicate with me. I asked for her daughter's contact details, as I knew she spoke excellent English, and we began corresponding. She told me that at 8 a.m. a few days earlier, Saru had dragged herself to the hospital for a PCR test, even though by this time, she was barely able to walk. By 3 p.m. she received the awful news that her test was positive.

Saru's family has a strong faith. Her husband moved from Okhaldhunga in the east to Kathmandu for university. He heard the gospel from fellow students who belonged to Campus Crusade for Christ. He and Saru attended the same youth group at Anamol Church in Lagankhel, and her parents and their pastors arranged their marriage in 1994. It was a Christian wedding, and Saru wore pink to integrate both a white Western/Christian dress and a traditional red Hindu wedding sari. Unfortunately, only her husband's father came from Okhaldhunga for the ceremony. His family was not happy that their son had become a Christian, nor that he was marrying Saru. Despite their displeasure, the wedding was still a joyous Christian celebration, and almost a hundred people attended.

Saru's daughter was born a couple of years later, and her son five years after that in 2001. Only then did her in-laws come to visit them, and family relations were gradually restored. When the deadly earthquake struck Nepal in 2015, Saru's in-laws' home and village in Okhaldhunga suffered considerable damage. As a consequence, her mother and father-in-law came to live with them in Kathmandu. After much prayer and faithful living, the two of them have become Christians, to the delight of Saru and her husband. Her daughter is also an avid student of theology and has contributed to Nepali books about the gospel, which Saru has proudly shown me.

This close-knit family was now experiencing the devastation of Covid together. Her son and daughter got away lightly and only had to endure a sore throat for a day. Her husband had a fever for three days, and her frail father-in-law had a fever and cough that lasted just under a week. Saru couldn't be sure if her mother-in-law became sick and laughingly told me it was perhaps only a sympathy headache. All of them were shocked by Saru's positive test result. When she became more and more breathless, they understandably began to panic. Saru was also refusing to eat, and this made them worry all the more.

On Saturday, when Saru messaged me to say she was sick, her family spent the day calling every hospital in Kathmandu to find her a bed. They also contacted all the oxygen providers advertising on social media in an attempt to obtain what they could to help her. By now, Saru had discovered that lying facedown on her bed enabled her to breathe more easily. Her situation was becoming desperate.

Just around the corner from Saru's home is Patan Hospital. It was not admitting Covid patients anymore because it was already packed, and oxygen was in such short supply. However, Saru's landlord was a doctor there, and he advised the family on which medicines to buy from a local pharmacy to treat her. They also purchased a small oximeter to fit on her finger to precisely monitor her blood oxygen level. A normal reading is 95 per cent, and in the UK, a reading below 92 per cent means that medical advice should be sought. Saru's oxygen levels were hovering between 75 per cent and 80 per cent.

Finally, at 6 p.m., an oxygen provider they had spoken to earlier in the day called to say that a canister containing ten litres of oxygen was available. The cost of the oxygen was 10,000 NRs (£70), but the family would also need to provide a deposit for the canister itself; this would cost 11,000 NRs (£77). In addition, they had to buy some other pieces of equipment, including the nose and mouth cover and tubing.

When the oxygen arrived, Saru's husband was then thrown into the role of nurse and doctor. Though he had no medical background, he had to decide how best to use the oxygen. Saru was begging for him to increase the oxygen flow, but he didn't want to use up the scarce supply too quickly. These decisions must surely be hard for doctors to make, but for a husband to watch his wife fight and plead for every breath must have been unbearable. He stayed awake the whole night praying for her and had to tend to her every need. She was unable to move; even the slightest change in body position brought on a coughing fit. Tenderly, he helped her go to the toilet using a bowl in her bed.

I asked Saru what was going through her mind during this period, and she told me that she declared victory over the virus in the name of Christ. She proclaimed that the blood of Christ had won her blood and that the virus, therefore, had no power over her blood. I am so encouraged by her faith, but she was by no means out of the woods yet.

The canister of oxygen only lasted until the morning. Yet, two miracles were about to occur. At this point in my interview with Saru, her daughter, who had been quietly sat next to her listening to our conversation, took over and enthusiastically relayed what happened next.

Saru's daughter teaches at a Christian school, and she had asked her fellow teachers to pray for her mum. At 6 a.m., just as the first canister of oxygen ran out, one of the teachers contacted her to offer another cylinder of oxygen. It arrived at the perfect time and was clearly orchestrated by God. The family were then able to return the initial canister in exchange for their deposit. So, when a hospice telephoned them the next day to offer a third cylinder, just when it too was required, they had the funds to pay for it. The timing was extraordinary, and Saru was sustained by the oxygen and prayers of everyone concerned for her.

Despite the miraculous provision of oxygen, it was still not enough, and it became apparent that Saru needed to be admitted to hospital. The medicine she had been prescribed was having little effect. Patan Hospital was still unable to take new Covid patients, and from news reports, it was evident that all other hospitals in the capital were full. It was then that Saru remembered Anandaban hospital. She breathlessly mentioned it to her husband, but he put her off the idea as Anandaban is a leprosy hospital.

Saru was born in Lubhu, a village in Kathmandu Valley that was several miles outside the ring road (which I discovered was already built in the 1970s, though there were barely any cars then). She is just a year older than me and, despite her family's poverty, was educated from the age of 4.

When her father was a teenager, he had contracted leprosy. The disease quickly caused his feet and legs to become infected as it was not common to wear shoes at this time. He heard about Anandaban Leprosy Hospital, which medical missionaries had established in 1957, and went there for treatment. While there, he met both Eileen Lodge and God, and quickly became a faith-filled Christian. Though not wholly cured, his leprosy became manageable. The staff at Anandaban taught him to care for both his physical and spiritual body.

Saru's mother was from central Kathmandu, and she met and fell in love with Saru's father. Although he had leprosy and was a Christian, both taboos, she was willing to marry him and settle in Lubhu. Nevertheless, after Saru's birth, it became challenging for her father to find work in the village because of the ostracism and discrimination he faced since he suffered from leprosy. Thankfully, UMN stepped in and offered her father a job and a place to live. The young family moved to Patan, where her father worked as a clerk for UMN. He delivered letters, and although he struggled to walk because of leprosy, he could use a bicycle, and they were patient with him. While working for UMN, his Christian faith flourished in the company of other believers.

Saru's grandmother also faced discrimination in the village because of her son's condition, so she joined the family in central Kathmandu. As she and her daughter-in-law witnessed the love and care for others that he imbued, despite society's maltreatment of him, both of them came to believe in Christ too.

Saru attended a government-run girls' school and was in the fifth class when she realized that a younger neighbour in the third class at a private school could read much more challenging books than her. Saru told her parents that she needed to swap schools, and they agreed. From then on, she went to a private co-ed school six days a week. On Saturdays, the whole family, including her younger brother, went to Gyaneshwar Church.

When Saru was 13 years old, there was a special programme at her church during which a visiting speaker spoke to the youth group. He explained that Jesus had come for every one of them and that each person needed to accept him for themselves. It was not enough to call themselves Christian just because they had been born in a Christian family. I find this teaching very forward-thinking; the gospel only reached Nepal in the 1950s. When Saru heard this talk in the 1980s, there were very few second-generation Christians to whom it was relevant. However, it was an important message, and Saru applied it. From then on, she had her own deep and personal relationship with Jesus.

Almost immediately, Saru's faith was put to the test. Her father was still regularly sick with leprosy and experienced a lot of pain. Saru would pray for him and often witnessed him get better in answer to her prayers. Her belief in God grew stronger and stronger. Since her parents had only received minimal education and she was literate, it fell on her to lead them during home Bible studies. This also helped her Christian faith to flourish.

Throughout her childhood, Saru had always been aware that Anandaban hospital was a place of hope and healing. Her father regularly visited for check-ups, and she knew he had been introduced to Christ there. As she cried out to God now, while suffering from Covid, she wanted to go to Anandaban hospital to experience that restoration and hope for herself.

Saru is Nina's sister-in-law, and Nina's husband works for Nepal Leprosy Fellowship. In desperation, Saru's husband called him to find out if Anandaban accepted Covid patients and if there was room for Saru. Regrettably, they were full, but Nina's husband made the staff aware that Saru needed a bed, and they prayed for her.

Eventually, three days later, the phone rang, and there was good news. A bed had become available at Anandaban hospital, and an ambulance would collect Saru and her husband at 11 p.m. that night. The admissions staff requested them to bring their own oxygen with them to the hospital in the ambulance.

When the ambulance arrived, Saru could not move, so her husband carried her on his back down the winding staircase and along twisting alleyways to the road. Her children carted two cylinders of oxygen that they had managed to procure.

On arrival at the hospital, they discovered another man in the bed allocated to Saru. He was staying at the hospital to take care of both his parents, who had come down with Covid concurrently. Though fast asleep, he graciously hopped out of bed, and without a change of sheets, Saru and her husband got in. They slept top-to-tail for the eleven days that Saru was in the hospital.

Under the hospital's care, Saru's condition gradually improved, and for the first time, she became aware of the broader Covid situation in Kathmandu. The gospel reached Nepal in the 1950s when the country opened up to foreigners. In the 1970s and 80s, young converts established the first churches, and now these same elderly pastors were succumbing to Covid on a daily basis. Lamentably, they had probably been visiting church members suffering from Covid and had not taken sufficient precautions. The Covid wave hit so suddenly; they were unprepared.

Nepali Christians regularly met on Zoom and YouTube to pray for the numerous pastors in hospital. Nevertheless, the Nepali church continued to lose some of its founding fathers. During the week that Saru was at Anandaban, the 96-year-old founder of Gyaneshwar Church died, and so did his son and successor, who was in his sixties. It was a frightening and discouraging time for all of Nepal's Christians.

For Saru at Anandaban, there were both blessings and struggles. The mother of the man who had been sleeping in her bed when she arrived was due to be sent home about a week later. Yet, the night before her discharge date, she suddenly collapsed and died. This lady had been eating and talking with Saru and was suddenly gone. In the hospital's other wards, the death rate was also high, and it was psychologically hard for Saru and her husband to witness so much death, suffering and sadness. Following the woman's death in her ward, Saru felt overshadowed by fear and wanted to leave the hospital as soon as she could.

Encouragingly, everyone in Saru's five-bed ward (but rather more people, as each bed was shared) was a Christian, and they prayed together. The atmosphere at Anandaban was loving, caring and permeated with the Holy Spirit. Saru's husband wandered the other wards, offering to pray for all the patients, including non-Christians. Most people gladly accepted his kind offer, and one man and his son gave their lives to Christ. Saru and her husband remain in touch with them, and when lockdown lifted, they planned to meet again at their church.

At the end of eleven days, Saru was at long last strong enough to go home. As she spoke to me of her time at Anandaban, I could see the emotion in her eyes. The hospital had not only saved her life, but, many years earlier, her father's as well. It had planted the seeds of the gospel in her family, leading to salvation for all of them. Consequently, she feels a deep spiritual attachment to the place. She is thankful for the loving Christian environment that welcomes every patient. When she was recuperating there, she heard similar stories from other patients who loved and appreciated Anandaban. In fact, at a later talk about the hospital, I heard that it is not uncommon for leprosy patients to poke and aggravate their leprosy wounds in an attempt to remain longer at the hospital.

When Saru arrived back at her home, I was desperate to visit her before I was evacuated, but could not do so because of the strict lockdown. So instead, I met up with her daughter in a quiet back road during the permitted shopping hours, and we prayed together briefly. We praised God for preserving the lives of everyone in their precious family.

Having passed through the eye of the Covid storm, Saru desired to give her life to share the gospel. She was still experiencing some breathlessness, but each day felt stronger, and she was hopeful that her facial swelling, as a result of being deprived of oxygen, would go down in time. It was evident to me when I interviewed her via Zoom that she wasn't her useful self. She and her husband were already in the habit of visiting distant villages on the rim of the Kathmandu Valley each Sunday (Nepali churches meet on Saturday) to share the gospel. She had renewed enthusiasm to continue this when she had completely recovered and her face no longer betrayed the effects of Covid. Saru gives the Lord every credit for saving her life and wants to spend her life serving him. She told me that earning money is inconsequential to her; instead, she longs to share her testimony and live as a witness to everything Christ has done for her.

Although Saru had recovered enough to leave hospital, the Covid situation in Nepal remained dire. For anyone above 50, Nepal was one of the worst places in the world to contract

Covid, as the death rate among this age group was the highest anywhere. The hospitals remained congested, and to make matters worse, no vaccines were on their way. Earlier in 2021, before the latter Covid wave, Nepal had managed to vaccinate one in 500 of the population, but few had received two vaccines. It looked as if the elderly would not receive their second doses, meaning the first dose would be rendered futile and the vaccination programme would need to begin again. Some countries, including the UK, were sending ventilators, but outside the major cities, there was a dearth of people trained to use them.

Among WWR's women, four had suspected Covid. One aged woman refused to have a Covid test because of the stigma surrounding it. Newspapers reported that Covid testing centres were busiest at night because Nepalis didn't want to be seen getting a test. Funerals are an essential rite within Nepali culture. If someone died with an official Covid diagnosis, rules prohibited the family from conducting all the rituals required for a proper funeral.

A woman and her daughter that WWR supports, who lived alone together, came down with Covid simultaneously and could not care for themselves properly. WWR's staff called them every day but could not do anything further to help, such as delivering food, because of the stringent lockdown. Thankfully, both of them pulled through in the end, but it was a worrying time for all of us.

The last of the four women to be diagnosed with Covid was Kopisha, whom I wrote about in an earlier chapter. She spent just four days in the hospital, and at one point, it seemed as if she had been discharged far too soon. However, she too slowly recovered and is now well.

The plan to evacuate all the spouses and dependents from the British Camp was eventually finalized. This decision was based not on the risk of Covid but on the chance that one of us may injure ourselves. For instance, a child might fall over and bang their head, and the overwhelmed hospitals in Kathmandu would not have the capacity to treat us. There were no available beds for any ailment among Kathmandu's hospitals, and any procedure requiring oxygen could not be performed.

At the end of May, I flew to RAF Brize Norton with around a hundred wives and children. Our plane was chartered by the MOD and was used to fly aid into Kathmandu before turning around to extract us. Our group was immediately bussed to a quarantine hotel in London, and we spent ten nights there in isolation. It was while staying at the hotel that I interviewed Saru on Zoom about her Covid experience. The army provided a house for me, and I lived there with two suitcases of belongings and no idea of when I would return to Nepal.

It was during our time in hotel quarantine that British newspapers began to report on a worrying new Nepal variant of coronavirus. This was misreported. Nepal does not have the capacity to sequence and identify Covid variants and relies on sending samples for additional testing to other countries on an ad-hoc basis. In May 2021, one of the samples it sent for testing was identified as the Delta/Indian variant. Due to the lack of regular sequencing, this variant hadn't been detected in Nepal before this, even though it was apparent to everyone that the Indian variant was rife. An Indian newspaper reported the discovery of a 'new' variant in Nepal, and this was wrongly picked up by British newspapers who thought it was different to the Delta variant. It wasn't; Nepal was simply catching up on identifying which variants were present in the country. Following reports of abuse directed at Chinese people soon after Covid was first detected, we hoped and prayed that this misreporting wouldn't lead to ethnically motivated ostracism of the Gurkha wives in their new communities.

Meanwhile, in Nepal, the country's incompetent government continued to argue between themselves and did little to help their country through the deadly Covid wave. Instead, in what has been called an act of 'political genocide', they called a general election for November 2021. Nepal's supreme court later judged that dissolving the government in this way was unconstitutional, and so the election was called off. It seems likely that Nepal's political class will continue squabbling for the foreseeable future and sadly, Nepal's people are destined to look after themselves as the country struggles through crisis after crisis.

Thankfully, no matter what is happening politically, there are beautiful witnesses to Christ's saving power present in Nepal. Saru is a beacon of light in a turbulent place, and her story is one of hope and rescue through faith in God. Her family is very ordinary, and I have seen her relate easily to Nepalis from all walks of life. I pray that her testimony of God's presence with her through suffering will bring life to many.

7

Campaigner: Maya

As I flew back into Kathmandu in early September 2021, I watched an unintentionally hilarious documentary about Stonehenge on the plane. The presenter set off towards Stonehenge with a steely expression and set jaw, bravely taking on the English drizzle and rolling hills. He cast himself as an intrepid explorer, and it was odd for me to see the familiar countryside through his eyes. Following my evacuation back to the UK in May, I had spent the summer with my children living in Larkhill, Wiltshire. Our bland and empty army quarters was just a couple of miles from Stonehenge, but every day I ached to return to Nepal. Though it was long and depressing, I had survived the summer and the bucolic landscape and was now heading back to where my heart belonged. I'm happy to report that the documentary presenter survived his time in Wiltshire too.

On arrival, Kathmandu was hot, humid and grey; heavy monsoon clouds hung over the valley. The dusty air clung to my skin, and within minutes I felt in need of a shower. Yet, though this might sound unpleasant, it was reassuringly familiar. I felt so happy to be back.

After one week of quarantine, my diary for the following week filled up, and I spent a hectic few days catching up with everyone I had missed. Unfortunately, my plans to see friends were delayed by twenty-four hours when I suffered an excruciating sting while walking in our garden; it may have been a scorpion, but I didn't catch a glimpse of what got me. At the time, it felt as if someone had plunged a knife into the top of my foot, and over the next forty-eight hours, my foot went from feeling as if it was being held over a fire to torturous itching. By the third day, though, it was almost entirely better, and I could go out and about after my long wait.

Seeing Saru for the first time was an incredibly joyful moment, and I was so glad to see that she was well again. The swelling on her face, one of the lasting side effects of Covid that had been so apparent when I interviewed her by Zoom, had gone down, and she was back to full strength. She described feeling breathless for most of the summer, but that had slowly eased, and she was healthy now. Over lunch, we identified four women that I wished to interview, and Saru arranged to contact them. I was eager to tell Maya's story because, unusually for the women we help, I knew she was in the middle of fighting a legal battle. When I had met her previously, she had shown herself to be brave and determined, and I wanted to understand how she became like that.

Just three days later, Saru and I set off in a taxi towards Maya's house. On our way, I took some videos of our journey to her home. These are available for readers to watch on YouTube (search for 'Come with me to Kathmandu – On our way to interview Maya'). As per usual, our journey took far longer than expected, the traffic was awful, and we got lost. Maya had suggested that we meet her at Krishna Mandir (temple), but there were two temples with that name in her neighbourhood. One was a large newly built bright pink temple on top of a hill. The other was an unfinished concrete structure barely distinguishable from the buildings around it. Of course, our taxi driver took us to the large new one, a well-known landmark within Kathmandu Valley, but Maya had meant for us to meet her at the small one. Once we discovered we were in the wrong place, we had to walk down a hill and up another to locate the Sano (small) Krishna Mandir. Two hours after setting out in the taxi, we finally met up with Maya, and we followed her down narrow lanes to her room.

We found Maya's 13-year-old younger son lying on one of the two pallet beds in her single-room home on the first floor of a shabby concrete apartment building. His school books were open, but he was playing a game on his phone. Like so many Nepali children, he was fed up with online school. He hadn't been able to attend in-person classes for the last eighteen months due to the pandemic. Maya sat down next to him on the bed, though she soon shifted to sit on the small patch of floor. I am amazed at how Nepali women seem so comfortable squatting on the floor; they can fit themselves into any space. I settled on the other bed, and there was a small stool for Saru to perch on.

Maya usually does domestic work for another household. She should have been working the day we met her, but she had arranged to work the following day and would not lose any pay for talking with us. We expressed our gratitude, and she told us that she had been doing domestic work since the age of 2. In fact, she couldn't remember a time when she didn't do household work.

From the outset of our conversation, it became apparent who Maya may have inherited her steeliness from. Born in Syangja, a district west of Nepal's tourist hub Pokhara, Maya was the only child born to her mother and father. Perhaps frustrated that her mother hadn't produced a son, her father brought home another wife one day. Just like that, Maya's mother divorced him. I asked her if this was an actual divorce on 'paper', and Maya confirmed that yes, it was.

Maya's father was a policeman, though this is more akin to serving in the army in Nepal. He was a drunkard and addicted to *raksi*, the local home-brew. As a result, he regularly beat her mother, so it was no surprise that she was eager to leave him. Making the separation official is unusual, though, as generally, this costs money.

Consequently, Maya and her mother returned to live in their *maiti gaon*, their maternal village. Maya was anxious to stress that they did not move back to their *maiti ghar*, their maternal home. Instead, they moved into an old empty house in the village where they did not need to pay rent. Maya's grandmother and great-aunt, who still lived in the maternal home, rejected her mother and were ashamed by the divorce. The two older women did nothing to welcome their young and vulnerable female relatives back to the village. Eventually, they died without having shown any love towards Maya. As she told me this, Maya wept.

To me, the older women's attitude is both saddening and unjust. I don't understand why they wouldn't want to help Maya and her mother after their escape from abuse. Maya's grandfather had already passed away, and it seems to me that the older women could have enjoyed the company of their granddaughter and great-niece. At the very least, having a younger woman live with them would have helped them do all the household chores necessary in rural Nepal. Instead, they allowed fear and shame to determine their actions rather than love. Though so many of these stories concern shame and honour, I still cannot fathom why they are such powerful forces in Nepal. Thankfully, I see signs of hope. In Bollywood films, watched avidly across Nepal, the hero often stands up to age-old prejudices. Though it is easier to be a hero on screen than in real life, I hope the enlightened attitudes in these films catch on.

Back in their *maiti gaon*, Maya and her mother had to provide for themselves, and worked relentlessly. Her mother became a labourer and carried a *doko* on her back at a construction site for a water channel project. She worked long hours, and Maya would prepare her mother's lunch before setting off to school. At the end of the school day, Maya would return home first so she would clean the house and prepare dinner before her mother came home. It was also Maya's responsibility to collect firewood from the jungle.

Attending school was fantastic for Maya, and for a while, she thrived. As the brightest in her grade, the teacher made her class captain, and she loved helping her schoolmates. Unfortunately, schooling is not free of charge in Nepal, and each pupil has to supply their own stationery. Maya had to make a single pen last for months, as her mother could not afford another. However, notebooks and paper were the hardest for her mother to provide. Maya required a notebook for each subject but had to make do with just one. Taking hold of one of her son's books, she showed me how she used every space on the page, including the footer, header and margins for her work. She wrote in tiny letters to eke out the most from every sheet.

One day she had a bright idea. While in the jungle over lunch, she collected yellow fruits called *lapsi*. These are called hog plums in English, although I have not heard of them before, and it appears that they only grow in Nepal. Upon discovering that her friends were eager to eat the fruit, she agreed to swap the *lapsi* for sheets of paper. After school, she sewed the sheets together to make a notebook. This bartering scheme was successful for several weeks until her friends' parents became suspicious about why their children were getting through so many notebooks. Regrettably, her friends were beaten by their parents, and they would no longer provide her with any paper.

By the end of sixth grade, her mother could not afford the school fees, which increased with each school year. Neither could she pay for any writing materials, so Maya's education ended, despite the protestations of her teacher, who didn't want to lose his star pupil. Instead, she took up livestock farming and began raising chickens and goats, which she sold for a small profit.

Maya's mother remarried at about this time, and they both went to live in another village with her new husband. Soon after, Maya's mother became pregnant and gave birth to a son. Sadly, the pattern of alcoholism and abuse repeated itself. The man beat Maya and her mother, though he eventually ran off, leaving Maya's mother on her own to raise two children. Once again, the small family returned to their *maiti gaon*, but by this time, Maya's grandmother had passed away. Since there were no male heirs, her mother inherited a small place to live. However, Maya's great-aunt was clever and had ensured that she kept hold of the best part of the property for herself.

Once Maya was 16 years old, her mother decided it was time for her to get married; as they were not members of a high caste there was no need for her to marry before this. Her mother put out feelers to their neighbours to ask if anyone knew of a suitable match for Maya. In a village a little way away, a family unknown to Maya and her mother were hunting for a wife for their son. They had five sons, and he was their second eldest. When a teenager, he had run off to Chitwan in Nepal's southern lowland region. Chitwan is hot year-round, and he lived on the street. On occasion, he would work as a labourer, but he spent everything he earned on drink. Now he was 30 years old; his family hoped to reform his character by arranging a marriage for him. At the time, Maya and her mother knew none of this. Though three other families had rejected him as a match for their daughters, regrettably, Maya's mother agreed to the pairing.

Maya and her husband were married at the local temple in a simple Hindu ceremony. She had not met him or even laid eyes on him before their marriage. His family were keen to secure a wife quickly before Maya's mother discovered the truth about him, and he was refused again.

Maya and her new husband were given gifts of cash from friends and relatives to celebrate their wedding, but her husband spent much of it that very day on alcohol. Whatever nerves Maya may have had about their wedding night were quickly laid to rest as her husband passed out. He was even more of a drunkard than her father, and she giggled as she told me that he was so drunk he peed all over their wedding bed. It must have been appalling for her at the time, but I sensed she pitied him now. I'm glad she can see the funny side too.

Just three days after their wedding, Maya's husband took off for Chitwan again, wanting a 'free life'. Maya was now left alone to live with her in-laws, who were more affluent than her own family. However, they were not as clean, and she told me with pride that though she had been poor as a child, at least her home had been clean. This household was the opposite. She tried to improve the family's cleanliness as much as she could, but it soon became apparent that it was a pointless exercise as everyone who lived there was dirty and messy. Her father-in-law was also a drunk, and without her husband around, Maya was treated like a servant; she worked from dawn to dusk.

After living like this for a year, Maya's mother-in-law decided that the two of them should go to Chitwan to find her miscreant son. An uncle lived in the area and knew his whereabouts.

However, it turned out to be easy to track him down as her husband was a well-known 'party animal' and local drunk. He was infamous for spending whatever money he had getting himself and his friends drunk. Maya and her mother-in-law took charge and brought him back to Syangja. Once again, he only stayed for three days, but it was long enough for Maya to fall pregnant.

While pregnant, Maya's in-laws did not treat her kindly. She had no money of her own, so she relied upon the family to feed her. They gave her two meals each day, but these contained barely any nutrients, and she felt delirious with hunger between meals. At mealtimes, she ate either *dhido*, a sticky mixture of flour and water, or stale rice and vegetable soup from the previous day's meals. The family could afford meat and fresh vegetables, but they told her that a daughter-in-law, even if pregnant, didn't get to eat them. Clearly, this impacted Maya; she revealed that if her sons ask her for meat now, she will always buy it for them, even if it means borrowing money to do so.

Every year, during the monsoon, *Teej* is celebrated by women across Nepal. Traditionally the festival is a time to fast and pray for one's husband, and women don their red wedding saris. Yet, according to anthropologist Elizabeth Enslin in her book *While the Gods Were Sleeping*, the night-time parties, solely for women, can also end up like raucous hen nights.[6] When she attended one, women put cucumbers between their legs and thrust at each other during erotic dances; she spent the evening fighting off groping hands. Men are strictly barred and spend the evening speculating about what the women are getting up to; in such a conservative society, I'm sure they would be shocked. Two days after interviewing Maya, I attended a *Teej* party with the British Camp at a swanky hotel. There was no groping nor cucumbers, but plenty of dancing and stunning saris. Nowadays the festival is an excuse to buy a new sari and all the accompanying jewellery and accessories. Most of the Gurkhas ladies spent the evening posing for photos.

Back in Syangja, Maya's mother came to collect her from her in-laws for the *Teej* festival. Tradition dictated that her mother had to ask permission to take her, but given that the festival was celebrated under the auspices of praying for one's husband, it would bring on ill fortune if her in-laws denied the request. After four days of celebrations, Maya went into labour while staying with her mother. They quickly set off on the hour and a half walk to the nearest bus route. After a further ninety minutes on the bus, they arrived at Gandaki hospital, on the outskirts of Pokhara. Maya spent twenty-four hours in labour before finally giving birth to a son at 9.30 a.m. He weighed 4.8kg (more than 10lbs) which is incredible given that Maya is tiny and at the time was so poorly nourished. No wonder she had spent her pregnancy feeling ravenous.

Maya's mother had deposited 2,000 Rs (£13) with the hospital to cover the delivery costs. However, when Maya's in-laws turned up to take her home, they took the 'change' from that amount. They didn't bring any food for Maya either. She wasn't provided with any food until the following evening, thirty-six hours after delivery, when she finally arrived home with them on the bus. Unsurprisingly, she fainted as she stepped down the bus's steps.

Throughout all this, Maya's husband was still in the dark about her pregnancy, and he had no idea that he was now father to a son. After living with her in-laws for a further year, Maya took matters into her own hands and decided to make the trip to Chitwan with her baby. They snuck out of the house and took a bus to Chitwan. Again, it was easy to track down her husband, but he was in an even more terrible state this time. A contractor he had been working for had beaten him, and he was lying on the street covered in blood. Maya showed her fortitude once more; she demanded that the contractor pay for her husband's medical treatment, then she searched for a room where they could live. She insisted that the two of them set up home together there in Chitwan. For a while, they would attempt to become a happy family.

Maya began selling vegetables from a *doko*, and her husband found work as a rickshaw puller. However, he had not changed and was still drinking most of their earnings. He also began beating her and, on one occasion, threw their young son across the room. Maya called the police, who arrested him. Not wanting to be associated with his bad behaviour, their landlord threw them out. There was no other option but to call her in-laws, who came to fetch their son from the police station and took them all back to Syangja. After a few days, her husband ran away again, and Maya was back to square one.

I've entitled this chapter 'Campaigner' because Maya does not give up and carries on fighting for herself and her sons, no matter what. She was determined that her son should receive an education and borrowed money from her mother to enrol him in school. Sadly, shortly after this, Maya became desperately ill; she simultaneously suffered from pneumonia, jaundice, typhoid and TB. I'm not sure this is possible, but whether true or not, she was doubtless exceedingly ill. Frustratingly, the money she had borrowed to put her son through school was wasted as while she lay sick in bed, none of the other family members bothered to take him to school.

In what was by now a familiar pattern, Maya's only hope was to return to her *maiti ghar*. Though sick, she managed to take her son and return to her mother, who took her to Fewa City

Hospital. She held up a fist to show me how thin she was when admitted. Fewa City is a private medical centre, but Maya still needed treatment after fifteen days there. The medical staff advised them to go to Gandaki hospital, a government facility that would be cheaper for them; she stayed there another fifteen days. In total, Maya's month-long treatment costs ran to 80,000 NRs (almost £600), and her mother took several loans to cover the bill.

Once discharged, Maya needed to continue taking daily medicine to combat TB for another eighteen months. Thankfully, TB medicine is available for free in Nepal. Since she lived so far from the hospital and could not visit daily, her doctor wrote a letter to their local health post permitting them to dispense the required medicine weekly. This allowed Maya to make the lengthy trip less often. After a year of living with her mother and taking regular medication, she was well.

It was time for Maya to make a new life for herself and her son. She knew there was no future for her with her husband or his family, and so she found a cleaning job at a school in Pokhara. Having enrolled her son in another school, she sold vegetables before and after her daily cleaning work to make ends meet. Though it sounds like she worked terribly hard, her face beamed as she described the freedom she felt. She was finally able to live life for herself on her own terms; when she was hungry, she ate.

Maya made friends with a man who also worked at the school and was around fifteen years older than her. He became a father figure to her and was kind to her son. It was good to know there was someone around on whom she could rely. Like many men, he had come to Pokhara for work. He supported a wife and family who remained in his village, but he lived in a hostel for most of the year.

After they had known each other for a few years, he went back to his village for the annual *Dashain* festival. He was away for a couple of weeks but called her regularly to see how she was faring. On his journey back to Pokhara, the bus he was travelling on broke down. It was past 10 p.m. by the time he reached Pokhara and very dark. He rang Maya from the bus, and she suggested that he come to her room to borrow her torch. His hostel was in a poorly lit part of the city, and it would help him find his way back.

When he arrived at her room, he gave her cucumbers and pickles from his village as a gift. I thought these were odd presents, and so did Maya; she laughed as she told me. However, his next words alarmed her. He informed her that he loved her and couldn't live without her. She had only ever thought of him as a kind-hearted friend, yet he said he had felt this way for a long time. She began to cry and reminded him that he was already married and she was not looking for another husband. She was happy taking care of herself. He continued to try to persuade her and falsely claimed that his wife had left him. He promised to care for her son and declared his willingness to endure any punishment from society and his family if he married her.

That night he stayed in her room since he would not leave. He raped Maya, yet though she wept quietly throughout her ordeal, she could not scream for fear of frightening her son, who was sleeping in the same room. She knew that no one would come to her aid even if she were heard.

In the morning, he got up and left for his hostel. The two of them avoided each other for the next month and did not speak, but then he wrote Maya a letter reiterating his love for her. Just days later, she discovered she was pregnant.

Maya's first instinct was to abort the baby. She was not a Christian at this time and given her experience with men, I'm not surprised she didn't want to take on the additional responsibility. She was barely making ends meet as it was and since she already had a son, she was no longer naïve about the difficulty of bringing up a baby independently. However, the man reassured her and told her not to worry. He said they were now 'one', and he would be there for her.

Maya had saved a small amount of money during her time in Pokhara and had managed to pay off the vast bill from her month-long hospital stay a few years earlier when she had TB. However, now they were 'one', the man's first act was to ask her for money, rather than doing anything to provide for her. Reluctantly she gave it to him, though he has never returned it. Since then, they have not lived together, but she now referred to him as her husband.

Eight months later, she gave birth to her second son in Gandaki Hospital. This time the hospital paid her 1,000 NRs to give birth under a nationwide scheme to encourage women to go to a hospital to deliver their babies rather than remaining at home. These payments have successfully reduced the maternal mortality rate in the country. Her new 'husband' was in the hospital for the birth, though he lied to his employer by saying his brother-in-law's wife was giving birth, rather than owning up to it being his child. He took Maya safely home afterwards to her room.

By chance, several visitors came to see Maya in the few months after her son's birth. First of all, her mother turned up and was shocked to discover she had a new grandson. Rather than getting angry with Maya, as might be expected, she was deeply concerned about her. The next visitors to arrive came from Maya's first husband's family. Her father-in-law had passed away, and they came to collect her so she could go back to the village to perform the funeral rites required of a daughter-in-law. When they saw Maya with a newborn baby, they no longer wanted her to come, but they wished her well.

Maya's second husband had big plans and decided to come to Kathmandu with his oldest son to establish a poultry farm and shop. He brought his first wife and family with him to help run the business and insisted that Maya come to the capital too so he could be close to his son. Maya agreed, hoping he would provide for them. He found a room for her and her two sons, where we were sitting on the day I interviewed her.

Meanwhile, Maya's younger half-brother, who had been raised with her following the end of her mother's second marriage, was now a migrant worker in Saudi Arabia. The two had remained close, and he was earning enough to send Maya some cash remittances. Knowing about this, her second husband turned up in her room with his son and first wife to demand money from her. Maya was outraged; the money was barely enough to support her and her sons, and she felt no obligation to provide for a family she hadn't willingly joined.

Over the years that I have run WWR, I have learnt many lessons. One of those is that, for a single woman, having helpful and reliable neighbours is more important than having a better room or more space. It turned out that Maya was now living in a good neighbourhood. Just yards from her room was Lila's house, and other sympathetic neighbours surrounded her. Apart from Lila, most of them were committed to worshipping the Hindu god Krishna (hence the nearby Krishna *mandirs*). Nevertheless, Lila explained the gospel to her, and she began to attend church when she wasn't working.

Encouraged by her neighbours, Maya decided to seek justice for her and her sons. First off, she approached a women's rights organization called Maiti Nepal; according to their website (see 'Further Resources' section), they have arbitrated more than 11,000 domestic violence cases. Maiti Nepal arranged for mediation sessions between Maya and her second husband. During these meetings, he promised to provide for his son and arrange a birth certificate. However, he took no action, and his assurances were worthless.

Frustrated by the lack of progress, once again, Maya took the initiative. She went to Lalitpur district court and boldly walked in. When she found the receptionist, she told her story and asked how to take her husband to court. The receptionist advised her to consult with LACC, so Maya made her way there. (On Maya's recommendation, we invited a women's advocate from LACC to visit WWR on International Women's Day earlier in the year – see Kopisha's story.)

LACC's small offices are located just behind my house near the British Camp in Manbhawan, and I can almost see into their rooms from my balcony. They are constantly busy, and Maya had to wait three months for an appointment. It was another three months before they were able to register her case with the district court. The first judge to look at her suit did a poor job organizing her papers, but thankfully he passed it on to a higher judge who took it seriously. Wonderfully, her neighbours and Lila were willing to be witnesses. They testified that Maya's second husband admitted to being her son's father and was not supporting them.

It was a huge relief when Maya won her case, but sadly her second husband is now, at time of writing, appealing at the higher court in Lalitpur. So far, the court has ordered him to divide his property between his sons from his first marriage and Maya's son, but there has been no progress with obtaining a birth certificate. For that, Maya will need to prosecute him at the court in his home town of Charikot, which will take time and money. Without a birth certificate, her son can't own property, so it's easy to see that her husband has little incentive to help organize one.

Meanwhile, Maya's faith has grown, along with the support and encouragement of her church. Regrettably, her older son, who is now 21 years old, has adopted the beliefs of their neighbours and is devoted to worshipping Krishna. He has prohibited Maya from getting baptized. She also fears that her neighbours will reject her if she publicly acknowledges her faith; she relies upon them for her home and work. Her younger son is a Christian, and I am encouraged that he is now a source of hope and strength to his mother, though he was conceived in such awful circumstances.

I know that Maya will continue to fight for justice for herself and her sons. My prayer is that she will be successful and that the journey to get there won't demand too much time and effort; she has little to spare. I hope she will find favour with each of the judges who look at her case. Having been maltreated by most men in her life, I also pray that her sons will break the cycle of alcoholism and abuse. As we departed her room, she told me that she lived for her sons and that they were what motivated her. I hope they honour her tenacity by loving and caring for her for the rest of their lives.

8

Mother: Maria

As a child in the eighties, I loved the Mr Men and Little Miss books. Their author, Roger Hargreaves, also wrote a series about animals that lived in Timbuctoo. The name intrigued me; from then on, I was eager to visit the real Timbuktu in Africa. As my reading broadened during my teenage years to include stories about Asia, the list of places I wanted to explore became longer and longer. I added Darjeeling, Jaipur, Kathmandu, Calcutta, Xanadu, Tibet, Kerala and Angkor Wat; I could go on and on, and I'm still hoping to visit many of them. Once I lived in Kathmandu, supposing that I could cross one place off my list, I soon started hearing a whole host of new and exotic-sounding places names. My list quickly became longer again. Among the new places that captivated me were the mysterious districts of Solukhumbu and Okhaldhunga. Of Nepal's seventy-seven districts, Solukhumbu is the one that borders Everest. I was desperate to go there; miraculously, my chance was about to arrive.

It's impossible not to have favourites among the women that WWR helps. Though I feel I shouldn't, some women are just delightful, and their stories change the way I think. Maria is one such woman; she's warm and energetic but also shy and humble. I've known her for ten years, and each time we see each other, she charms me a little more.

Maria had spent eight years living at our first women's home, Anugraha Ashram in Godavri, south of Kathmandu, where she had taken care of our cow and was a dab hand at kitchen gardening. She never sat still. Two years ago, she returned to live in her home district of Solukhumbu. Her son, whom I was not even aware of, was now grown up. He asked her to return to him and his sister, who I also did not know existed, and they promised to care for and protect her. Maria's story is dark and distressing, but her son is a hero, and there is a fairy-tale ending. I was keen to include it, and so to Solukhumbu I went.

We hired a car from Kathmandu for our four-day adventure and set off early one Sunday morning. Esther, her husband, and Saru also joined me on the trip. The journey to Salleri, where Maria now lives, is eleven hours by car. We would take our time to get there across two days but attempt to drive back in just one day.

The first six hours of the journey took us along a winding road that clung to the edge of the Sunkoshi River. We were travelling during the tail end of the monsoon, and our driver had to pick his way across mudslides and rockfalls high above the roaring waters as we edged along the valley. Having crossed the river using a newly built bridge rather than the ferry that was once the only way across, we climbed upwards along hairpin roads and into the clouds to Okhaldhunga. We spent our first night there, but the less said about that guest house, the better; needless to say, we won't be going back.

Following a breakfast of spicy samosas in the morning, we took what should have been a short detour off the main road. Unfortunately, our front tyre became stuck in a hole where a drain cover was missing. Thankfully, Esther's husband summoned some help from the local village, and together we lifted the car out of the hole. There was still time to visit my friend who works at UMN's hospital in Okhaldhunga. She and I had been part of the same Zoom Bible study group for the previous year, during the coronavirus lockdown, but had never met each other in person. It was great to take a hospital tour and see the fantastic work they do in such a remote location.

Having rejoined the main road, we climbed upward again and crossed the border into Solukhumbu. It felt much colder when we stepped out of the car to take photos of the prayer wheels and flags that marked the border. We had passed a procession of scruffy monks and male family members carrying a body on a bier on our way up; they were a Tamang funeral procession. The corpse had been arranged on the stretcher in a cross-legged seated position rather than lying prone. Esther explained that the body was posed like this to mimic Buddha's position when he received enlightenment. The corpse would be buried like this.

As we descended into Salleri, the road became steadily worse, there were more rock and mudslides, and we had to ford streams that ran across the road. Ahead of us, though, a stunning valley vista was unfolding. The name Salleri derives from the word for pine trees, and they surrounded the town, giving the place an alpine feel. Salleri is perched on one side of a valley, and the opposite side rose vertically in front of it. It was possible to look across at the opposite side from anywhere within the small town as if it were a giant widescreen television. I could have stared at that view for decades.

We pulled to one side at a busy intersection by the district post office and rang Maria; she came out to meet us, and there were smiles all round. We followed her on foot along the busy bazaar and down a hidden flight of steps to the restaurant that her family runs. Having settled us, Maria disappeared but returned a few minutes later with her newborn grandchild in a woven cot on her back. It was suspended from her forehead in the same way a *doko* is. We marvelled at the contraption, and Maria beamed. Her granddaughter was just 4 months old and had been born following an eight-year wait. Maria described how she had carried her children in *doko*-cots after their births. However, it had been far more strenuous for her then, since she had been expected to plant rice and carry on with farming work while lugging the heavy cradle. Nowadays, she did some household chores while carrying the little girl, but nothing as demanding as before.

It would be another twenty-four hours until we would be able to interview Maria. Before then, she was needed to babysit her granddaughter. Her daughter ran the busy restaurant and had plenty of customers to attend to. In the meantime, the four of us from Kathmandu toured the town and climbed up into the hills. We also settled ourselves at a traditional yet spotlessly clean guest house across the road.

After lunch the following day, we crowded into Maria's room to hear her life story. The room's walls were painted bright white, but there was no window to let in light. We entered the room when the sun was shining brightly, but it was dark and foggy when we came out. It was as if we went from summer to winter in one afternoon.

Maria was born in 1970 in Kaku village, a two-hour bus ride up and east from where we sat. Looking at the place on Google Maps, countless narrow rice terraces indicate an extremely steep terrain. Roads snake back and forth as they zigzag up to the tiny settlement. Maria is illiterate and innumerate, there were no calendars in her impoverished village, and hence her idea of dates and years is very vague. She had an older brother, who has since died, but has no idea how many years older than her he was.

When her mother gave birth, it was out of doors beside the river on the way back from a day of farm labour. It cannot have been an easy birth, and Maria knows little about it. However, when Maria was just 4 months old, her mother died, perhaps from a complication due to childbirth, given that neither of them received any medical care. Maria's father remarried quickly, as would have been the norm, and so Maria was raised by her stepmother, who she said loved her. A younger brother was born sometime afterwards.

Neither Maria nor her older brother received any education, though her younger brother had a few years of schooling. When Maria asked to attend school, she was reprimanded; her father asked, 'Who will work if you go to school?' At about the age of 7, she hid outside a literacy class and spent a few hours listening to the lessons. When her father found out, he beat her with stinging nettles.

At the age of just 5, Maria was forced to participate in the *goth nikalne*, or 'sending to the cowshed' tradition. Young children were sent up the mountainside on their own to live and care for a cow. They would have to fend for themselves for six months before returning home to do agricultural work. Maria told me that the cowshed her family sent her to was fifteen minutes from home, but I expect it would have been closer to an hour away for my weak Western legs. She slept on the straw, and her mother or father visited every few days with flour. Not knowing what to do with the flour, young Maria had to work out how to cook it. She foraged for vegetables among the fields and, at times, was desperately hungry. I'm convinced that she must have been severely malnourished; Maria is only a little over 4ft tall, whereas her children are at least 5ft, even the girls. I asked her how she felt while living in the cowshed. She said she was dreadfully scared: scared of the cow wandering off, scared of her father beating her if something happened to the cow, and scared of being alone.

As I listened to her description of *goth nikalne*, I could barely believe what I was hearing, and neither could Saru and Esther. We were each in shock that 5-year-olds had to do this, but I expect it may be a tradition that continued for generations. Perhaps David, in the Bible, was also banished to the fields for an extended period and forced to grow up quickly. Thankfully, Maria told us the practice has stopped now. Praise God.

When she was 10 years old, her father decided to put Maria to work for other families. Their family cow stayed at home, where Maria longed to be, and she left to live in other mountaintop cowsheds. In return, her father received grain from the other families; the village economy hinged on bartering rather than cash. This work would soon stop, though; at just 12 years old, Maria was wedded. Though not from a high caste, her family and tribe, both of which were extremely traditional, believed it was essential to marry girls off before their periods began to guarantee purity.

Maria could not tell me what religion she practised as a child. They received white *tikas* (coloured grains of rice placed on the forehead) rather than the more common red powder *tikas* seen across southern Asia. She took part in a few festivals and rituals but had no idea of their significance. The area she lived in was so remote that no one could read, and there was no sacred text; everything they knew about religion was founded on hearsay and superstition.

As a result of this lack of religion, Maria's wedding ceremony was pragmatic and traditional rather than religious. One day, the groom's family turned up with home-brewed *raksi* and a leg of pork. Had they been wealthier, they would have brought a whole pig. They presented these gifts to Maria's parents and asked permission for her to marry their 16-year-old son. Her parents consented, and each of them, including Maria, had a slug of *raksi* to confirm the union. They shared the pork leg between the two families as the wedding feast. Maria left that same day to live with her new husband and in-laws.

I asked whether her parents ever did the same and invited a girl to marry her older brother in this way. Unusually, he refused to take a wife as he felt too ashamed of his poverty and believed it would be a sin to force a girl to marry him when he couldn't provide for her. Sadly, her brother died aged 45 without having married. He was a porter and collapsed while carrying a heavy load up steep terrain.

Shortly after her marriage, while she was still only 12 years of age, Maria ran away with a friend whose mother had just died. They were both searching for peace. They walked for three days and travelled from their village to Phalpu, Kinja and on to Jiri, where they caught the bus to Kathmandu. Once they reached the capital, they found work at a carpet factory in Baisepati, no more than a couple of miles from my house in Manbhawan and close to where Suki now lives. A family from their village ran the factory. After a month, though, her friend advised her to go back, fearing that Maria's in-laws would blame her for taking their new daughter-in-law away from them.

A year or two later, Maria's period arrived. Although still unclear about her religion, she was not permitted to cook or enter the *puja* (worship) room while menstruating. Her farm work continued, though.

For the next few years, she and her husband barely saw each other. He was a stonemason and worked for weeks at a time in various villages across Solukhumbu. However, she went much further afield. In another rite of passage for teenagers in Solukhumbu, she became a porter. She was younger than my daughter when she began carrying loads from the Terai, the stretch of land that runs along Nepal's southern border, to the mountain towns in Solukhumbu. Most of the Terai is extremely hot and less than 100ft above sea level. At the end of her arduous journeys were places such as Namche Bazaar and Lukla, at around 10,000ft above sea level. There were countless mountain passes in-between, one of which we had journeyed over, that took us above the clouds.

One of Maria's main tasks was to carry rock salt pieces, which must have been extremely heavy and jagged, from the Terai to the mountains. While I write this, I'm glancing at the sky outside my window. I cannot imagine what it must have been like for a teenager to carry such loads day after day up into the clouds. As a porter, each day began at 4 a.m. and did not finish until 6 p.m. The journey to Namche took ten days, and although she would walk with friends, there were many times when she cried because of the pain. Her only clothes were those she wore, and to keep her warm at night, she had an old woollen blanket that had been handmade in her village.

Around five years after her marriage, Maria fell in love with another man; they had met during her journeys to other towns, but he was from the same village as Maria and her husband. Maria returned to her first husband and told him he was not handsome enough for her and she was leaving him. Her in-laws begged her to stay, and interestingly they claimed they had treated her well because they had provided her with gold and a *doko* strap to go across her head. A strap was considered a valuable asset since it meant she could work and had a trade.

Soon after, her husband guessed that she had met someone else. They had a long argument during which he threatened to cut her head off with a *khukri* knife – these knives are used daily all over Nepal, but have been made famous by the

Gurkhas. Maria exposed her neck to her husband, daring him to cut her. He knew that her boyfriend was a Christian, so he asked, 'Why do you want to be with him? Christians are lower than the lowest caste.' The fight ended when she removed her *bulak*, a gold nose ring and *dhungri*, a gold coin attached to her ear. She had worn both since marrying him. Finally, she took off her *pote*, the beaded marriage necklace, and threw it in his face before storming off. These actions were akin to telling her husband she was divorcing him.

Maria was already aware of Christianity. The first native Christian missionaries reached Solukhumbu in the 1970s, and Gyaneshwar Church in Kathmandu had planted a small congregation in her village shortly afterwards. She had gone to tea with her boyfriend's uncle as a child, and they had said grace. At the time, she had asked what they were doing, and the family had explained that they were Christians and needed to thank God for providing them with tea. This explanation made sense to Maria.

While married to her first husband, she had skipped her farm work one day to stand outside the village church while a service took place. She heard the sermon and the songs, and it felt good to be there. The pastor said they would gain nothing by worshipping trees and stones; these inanimate objects couldn't change anything, and they didn't speak. She already thought that her folk Hindu religion was a sham; she had observed how the *raksi* they seemed obliged to make was harmful to people. There also seemed to be endless demands for money to pay for *puja* and the witchdoctor's help. She was eager to give these up and become a Christian instead.

Maria and her new 'husband' never officially married. His parents were already dead, so there was no one to object to them living together. His brother and sisters accepted the love match, so they began their new life together as if they were a married couple. They went to church regularly and were baptized as soon as possible.

The church was called Sagarmatha Ishai Mandali, which means Everest Believers' Church. Services had to be held in secret when opposition to churches increased during the 1980s. The church had just under thirty members, and most suffered persecution at this time. One day, the pastor's family was beaten. The pastor himself was hit over the head, which cracked his skull, but mercifully he survived.

When Maria left her first husband, this had disgraced her maternal family, and they were no longer speaking to her. However, a few years later, her father became sick. Although they had ostracized both Maria and her new husband,[7] her husband visited his in-laws, explaining that he had to show God's love to them and that her father mustn't die without going to church. Once they had accepted her new husband into their house, he brought Maria with him when he next visited. Maria's aged father was an amateur witchdoctor himself by this point, and his home was full of artefacts used for his invocations. Maria and her husband prayed for him and explained that he should destroy these artefacts since they wouldn't help him. Miraculously he agreed to burn them, and after they prayed, he was healed and believed in God. Even now, Maria cannot believe how easy his conversion was.

The other villagers knew that Maria's father had burned his witchdoctor regalia; it was impossible to hide it from them. They badgered him in the weeks following his conversion, telling him that only poor people became Christians. By the time Maria revisited him, the villagers had turned her father against Christianity. Her parents scolded her for making them destroy all the accessories that had provided them with a source of income.

Some villagers came to visit the house while Maria was still there, so she hid upstairs. She coughed at one point, and the villagers challenged her father to call her down so they could beat her. Her father denied she was there, and she escaped like a cat out of an upstairs window. Following this, her parents realized how foolish and cruel the village beliefs were and became Christians again, though in secret.

Maria and her handsome husband had two children together, a son and a daughter, and were happy. However, he had been in poor health since they first began living together. He worked in construction, and regrettably, he developed throat cancer. It may have been dust from the sites he worked on that triggered it, or he may have been genetically vulnerable. Asian males have a high risk of forming cancerous cells in the throat[8] if they chew betel, a common habit across Asia; tobacco is wrapped in a betel leaf and placed under the tongue next to the gum.

After ten years together, he passed away, and Maria was devastated. They had spent the little money they had on his treatment, so by the time he died, not only had the family lost their breadwinner, but they were utterly destitute. Thanks to the kindness of her deceased husband's family, some of whom were Christians, Maria managed to continue living in their village. However, she was reviled by most of the villagers; not only was she a Christian, but she was also landless now, and they blamed her for her husband's death. In their superstitious minds, bad things only happen to those that deserve them, so she was held responsible for her husband's fate.

A man in the village kept on badgering Maria and making lewd comments. She told him that she had children and it would be inappropriate for her to be with him. His obscene behaviour went on for several months, and eventually, he brutally raped her. Sadly, it was not a one-off, and he raped her several more times. Although she tried everything to avoid him, he would catch her unawares while she worked on remote terraces.

Nature took its course, and in the end, she became pregnant. Once her baby bump was visible, the villagers insisted she explain who the father was. So, she told them that this man had repeatedly raped her. In more developed countries, it's accepted that a child's father should take responsibility for some of the costs of raising a child, no matter the circumstances of its birth. Usually, a father can be tracked down by an identification number, and he pays child support from his income. None of this is possible in Nepal; in remote villages such as Maria's, no centralized administration can make a father responsible for his children. Instead, the village leaders took matters into their own hands and compelled the rapist to take Maria into his home and care for her. Essentially, the two of them were forced to marry.

Initially, the man's family agreed that Maria could bring her son with her. Sadly, they would not accept her daughter, so she remained with Maria's sister-in-law from her second 'marriage'. Maria gave birth to a daughter shortly after joining her new family. Both the man and his parents were cruel to Maria, and they treated her like a slave. In the end, they rejected her son, too, so he went to live with his Christian uncle.

Maria's husband would often become drunk, and her in-laws told her she would be to blame if anything happened to him. He ran away up the hill to a cowshed on one occasion, and she found him there drunk and enraged. She begged him to come home as she knew her in-laws would take it out on her if he didn't. He suddenly took out a *khukri* and tried to strike her with it; she only stopped him by catching the *khukri* in her bare hands. At the same time, she was carrying their small daughter. The two of them fought like this for three hours.

Having nowhere else to go, Maria spent several miserable years living with this family in constant fear of the next assault. Her in-laws were also unhappy with their impoverished situation and eventually persuaded their son to find a job abroad. When he left to go overseas, they threw Maria and their grand-daughter out of the house.

Penniless and distraught, Maria didn't know what to do; she had to find a way to feed her daughter. She asked around for work, and a sympathetic Sherpa family took her in. They paid her 50 NRs (35p) each day to look after their cow and dig potatoes on a steep mountainside. We had passed Bagam, the village where this Sherpa couple lived, on our way to Salleri. It was at the top of a mountain pass, and clouds hung over it all day long. On our way home the following day, we would trudge up muddy potato fields in our failed attempt to watch the sun rise over the mountains. The mud was red and claggy; it would have been gruelling and filthy work for Maria.

Word reached Maria's sister-in-law (her second husband's sister) that she was no longer living with the family of her rapist. This sister-in-law, though not a Christian, was already taking care of Maria's elder daughter, so she came to fetch Maria and took her back to live with them in Salleri. Her sister-in-law promised Maria that though she would need to do some household work, nothing more arduous would be expected from her. Living in Salleri also meant that her youngest daughter could attend school. Maria proudly told me that she enrolled her in school when she was just 3 years old.

When they got to Salleri, the reality was different for Maria. Soon after she began living with her sister-in-law, the list of jobs the family expected her to do grew longer and longer. Though Maria despised it, she had to make and serve *raksi* at her sister-in-law's small inn. The family was wealthy and owned forty mules used to carry goods into the mountains; Maria was also expected to care for them. The work was relentless, but what upset her most was that she was kept so busy she couldn't go to church.

Maria began to pray fervently for the opportunity to go to church and be with other Christians. Meanwhile, 5,000 miles away, the trustees of WWR and I felt called to open a women's home for our neediest and most vulnerable women. Frustrated with the lack of safe housing in Kathmandu, especially the shortage of rooms with reliable water and electricity supplies, we had begun to seek God about whether he wanted us to open a place of our own. One of our trustees worked closely with an international non-governmental organization (INGO) in Kathmandu. Due to a change in focus, they no longer needed the use of a training centre on the outskirts of the Kathmandu Valley that they owned and were willing to rent to us.

I was initially very reluctant to take on the property; it seemed enormously expensive and more than we needed since it was on a large piece of farmland. At the time, I lived in military housing in Portsmouth, close to the port and with views across to the Isle of Wight. I had dismissed the training centre, but following days of mist and the constant sound of foghorns, God woke me up in the middle of the night and prompted me to look out of the window. The fog had vanished, and the view across the waters of the Solent was crystal clear; every light in the town of Ryde was visible. At that very moment, God told me I was seeing clearly now, and WWR should rent the training centre from the INGO.

A few weeks later, Nepal's country director for the INGO was in London for the organization's annual conference. Two other trustees and I met him at the hostel where he was staying and spent several hours looking over floor plans and discussing plumbing, cesspits and cowsheds. By the end of our conversation, he had answered all our questions, and we were ready to sign the lease. WWR was about to open our first women's home, Anugraha Ashram.

Anugraha Ashram would require staff, so Esther invited Hitu (introduced in Somi's story) to oversee the place. Excited at the prospect of her new job, Hitu asked some women at her church to pray for her and to attend the opening celebration. One of these women was from Salleri and told her sister, who still lived in the town, about our plans. This woman knew Maria and passed the news of our home on to her. I am staggered by God's intervention and was unaware that word of our women's home had reached such a remote district. At the time, WWR was a small charity supporting no more than forty women, and I had assumed no one knew of it. We needed to keep news of our work quiet due to the sensitive circumstances of our women. However, God had different priorities and ensured Maria found out about our plans.

Maria was thrilled to hear about a Christian woman's home and was eager to join us, but leaving Salleri would mean leaving her two teenage children behind. In truth, as a widow, she had already lost access to and control of them. Her second husband's uncle determined her son's path in life, and her daughter worked for her sister-in-law. It was a choice between them and furthering her relationship with God. She concluded that she would rather die than go back to Hinduism. Hence, she accepted God's invitation to live at our women's home in Kathmandu. God was faithful to her choice and did not let her children slip away from him either. Though the family was physically separated, he upheld each of them and continued to work in their lives.

One night, Maria and her youngest daughter, who was 5 or 6 years old, slipped away from the house in Salleri; they had no belongings to take with them. Carrying her daughter on her back, Maria walked for three days until they reached Jiri, where the two of them caught the bus to Kathmandu. The bus travelled along winding roads up and down hills and valleys; Maria spent most of the trip vomiting. Once they arrived in Kathmandu, she spent another three days with her head spinning, weak and unable to eat. By the third day, she was starting to feel more normal. It was the day of the opening celebration at Anugraha Ashram, WWR's Grace Women's Home. She travelled with Hitu and some church members in a minibus to the outskirts of the Kathmandu Valley where the home was located for the inauguration party. When the celebrations were over, she didn't board the minibus to return to central Kathmandu and remained with us for the next eight years.

As Maria looked about at the small fields surrounding the home, she was desperate to begin farming them; she asked Hitu if she could start immediately. Regrettably, she was too unwell to commence the work. Days after Maria joined us, she was diagnosed with tuberculosis, and WWR arranged hospital treatment for her. Once she was well, she began planting crops in the fields but soon thought she had made a mistake by coming to us. The terrain around the home was very different to what she was used to. Since the altitude was far lower than that of Solukhumbu, it was, therefore, much hotter. She didn't like the leeches and the occasional snakes but soon became competent at hitting them over the head to kill them. On one occasion, the ladies heard a mountain leopard growl at them from nearby. To keep everyone safe, WWR employed a *chowkidar* (guard) to watch the home overnight, and no one was harmed.

Maria developed an incredibly close relationship with Somi and still speaks to her every day on the phone. She feels as if Somi's son is her own and remembers when the two of them arrived at Anugraha Ashram just days before the big earthquake.

When I visited the women's home during those years, I remember meeting a beaming lady who proudly showed me the neatly planted fields and the well-loved cow. On one occasion, her daughter led the day's Bible study and prayers. I was delighted that God had redeemed her situation so thoroughly; a child born due to rape now led others in worship.

Throughout Maria's stay at our women's home, I had no idea that she had two other children waiting for her in Solukhumbu. However, she remained in touch with them. In 2019, her son, a youth pastor, invited her back to live with them. He had been worried for her throughout his teenage years and had always been very thin; now she is back with him, he is putting on weight. Maria's rapist husband is still alive and in the area; she needs the strength and protection of her son to endure living near that man again.

Though not raised in a Christian home, Maria's elder daughter fell in love and married a Christian man in the intervening years, so she too is now a strong Christian. God was faithful to Maria, and though she had to leave her older children while she lived with us in Kathmandu, he preserved their bonds and faith; he is a good God.

Maria's younger daughter believes that her father is Maria's loving and handsome second husband. The family has worked together to obtain a birth certificate and citizenship for her in his name. Nowadays, they live together in Salleri and dote on the newest addition to the family, Maria's granddaughter. They attend church together, and when Maria's son visits other churches to preach, she watches his sermons on YouTube.

Following my interview, we were each in floods of tears. There is still some sadness in Maria's life as she desperately misses us in Kathmandu. Having spent eight years living with her friends at Grace Women's Home, it is terribly hard for her to live eleven hours away. She had been praying that someone would visit her and was so excited when she found out we were coming that she hadn't slept for days. That evening, her family invited us to dinner at their restaurant and treated us to a delicious *dal bhat* (rice and lentil meal). They presented us with gifts to thank us for caring for their mum, and it was truly humbling. God deserves all the glory. Maria's story demonstrates how he works in so many ways that we are unaware of. Throughout the meal, we each shared our testimony, and there were many more tears. As we left, our prayer was for us to meet again.

In the morning, we woke at 3.30 a.m. to return to Kathmandu. The hairpin mountain passes we had driven along to reach Salleri were even more terrifying in the early morning darkness. Sadly, our plans to watch the sun rise over the mountains from a hill peak at 6 a.m. were dashed when the clouds didn't clear. To amuse us on our journey, we watched crowded buses carrying flocks of goats on their roofs traverse slick mud landslides. Thankfully all the goats survived, and so did we; having made good progress, we were back in Kathmandu twelve hours after setting off.

My heart broke as I left Maria and Salleri, and I have no idea if or when I will see her again. I know that she prays, and God has always acted in her life to keep her close to him. No matter what happens, I am confident that he has good plans for her and her family, and I am excited to see what the future holds for her granddaughter, growing up in a close-knit Christian family. 'The kingdom of God belongs to those who are like these' (Mark 10:14), and I am grateful that I have had a ringside seat to observe God at work in such loving and majestic ways through Maria. The entire Solukhumbu region is blessed because of God's presence with her.

9

Winner: Binsa

On our return journey from Salleri, we had followed several buses carrying flocks of goats on their roofs. These animals had no idea that their journeys would be one-way only. During the festival season in Kathmandu Valley, 3.5 million goats are slaughtered each year. Countless buses bring live farm animals into the capital from across rural Nepal.

The first celebration of the season is *Dashain* (known in India and the UK as *Dashera*). The British Camp marked this with a party, *dal bhat* feast and traditional dancing show. All of the ladies, including the British wives, wore saris, and we were patiently helped to get dressed by the obliging Gurkha wives. The Buddhist lama and Hindu pundit were also invited to the camp to perform *puja*, bestow *tikas* on foreheads and sacrifice a goat. Thankfully, as Christians, my husband and I were allowed to decline to take part in these rituals. Still, many of the British soldiers embraced these traditions.

The *Dashain* festival lasts fifteen days, then just one week after it ends, *Tihar* begins. *Tihar* is the festival of lights and is better known around the world as *Divali*. Houses are covered in strings of lights, and during dark evenings, it is fun to walk through Kathmandu's streets to look at them. Outside each house, a *rangoli* is made on the ground. These are circular patterns made of coloured powder. In the middle of each *rangoli*,

Nepalis place offerings to the Hindu god Lakshmi. This god is famed for bestowing material blessings, and a line of paint leads from the *rangoli* into the house to show Lakshmi where to go. To me, the *rangolis* are like a more elaborate version of the 'Santa stop here' signs that some people place in their gardens at Christmas. As I looked up to admire the lights on each house, I also had to remember to look down to avoid walking on the *rangolis*; they were definitely a trip hazard. On camp, the staff played traditional *Tihar* gambling games under the supposedly watchful eye of Lakshmi, whom they believe helps favoured players win.

The festival period can be a difficult time for Nepal's Christian believers. Refusing to take part in the *pujas* and *tika* blessing ceremonies can invoke the wrath of their families. Hinduism is characterized as a fear–power religion, and devotees appease the gods through *puja*, which involves making numerous offerings. There are no worship or teaching services that we would recognize. Consequently, when a Nepali person becomes a Christian, their family members are immediately fearful that the Hindu gods will become angry. Regrettably, they take out their fear and anger on the convert. The festival period can also leave many Nepalis in debt, spending too much on food and gifts for their families, as is the case for many people who celebrate Christmas. In addition, the gambling traditions at *Tihar* compound these problems, and Nepalis can bet huge sums and lose.

The festival season falls at the end of the monsoon when the fields are greenest and the air clearest. On the day Saru and I took a taxi to visit Binsa, there was a glorious Himalayan panorama. As we drove up the edge of the valley, the view became more and more picturesque. On reaching her room, I realized I had visited the place before as Binsa lives where Hitu used to be. Low concrete buildings surround a small market garden, and the yellow flowers of the mustard oil plants were blooming. It turned out there was even a view of the mountains from her squat toilet, thanks to some gaps in the brick wall that surrounded it.

Binsa was born in Taplejung, a mountainous district in the far east of Nepal next to the Indian and Tibetan borders. Though she is from a high-caste family, her household was exceptionally poor. At one time, they had owned land, but her father had sold it to make ends meet. The man who now owned their land paid piecemeal for it; he would give them cash as and when he felt like it. There was nothing her family could do to change this since they had no power over him.

Binsa was the youngest of five children. Her parents often had to leave their offspring to fend for themselves while the two of them worked as porters. Their work involved carrying cement and sand to towns in the area, generally no more than two days away. Without their parents around, the children practised no religion and did not perform *puja* in the house. Their only participation in any religious activity was when they attended celebrations during the annual *Dashain* and *Tihar* festivals.

Neither Binsa nor her brothers and sisters attended school. As the youngest, Binsa enjoyed her childhood and got away with doing very little. In many ways, her formative years were idyllic. She spent most of her time playing, and it wasn't until she was 12 years old that she began to carry out household chores, late by Nepali standards. She started by cutting grass for their cow and cleaning the kitchen. Her least favourite errand was collecting and carrying cow dung to fertilize their crops.

Binsa also managed to escape the rigours of *chhaupadi* and the onerous rituals that should have come with her first period. In what seems to me to be a good tactic, she simply didn't tell anyone when she began menstruating, and by the time of her second period, it was too late to mark it. Her family made her stay indoors during each of her periods, but that was the only restriction. Her happy childhood continued.

At the age of 15, Binsa fell in love. A government engineer from Syangja, in western Nepal, was overseeing an irrigation and drinking water project in her village. Though he was almost twice her age, they began meeting in secret. He bought gifts for her, and despite strongly suspecting that he was already married, she was just a teenager and could not resist him.

Binsa did not know how babies are conceived, but within a year, she was pregnant. She was also ignorant of what it meant when her period stopped, so her mother and neighbour were the first to work out she was pregnant. They noticed that she was rapidly putting on weight and put two and two together. Thankfully, her parents were not angry with her; instead, their main concern was to know who the father was.

By the time Binsa knew she was pregnant, her seducer had already left for Chennai in India to continue his training. They wrote to each other, and he knew about the pregnancy. Unusually, he expressed a desire for a girl since he already had two sons with his legal wife. Binsa's parents also did not mind if the child was a boy or girl. Consequently, she did not experience the anxiety and pressure to produce a son that most women in Nepal endure. When the time came, she gave birth to a healthy boy.

The baby's father was in Chennai for a year, so their son was already 3 months old when he returned. He accepted the child and spent a week with Binsa before returning to India. Though he seemed happy with them both, he left no money with Binsa to help bring up their son, so the burden of raising him fell entirely on her.

The two of them continued to correspond. After another three years, he returned for a short visit to Jhapa, directly south of Taplejung on the Terai. Binsa's father escorted her and her son to meet him and left them there to spend three days in his company. They had a romantic time together and barely left their hotel. Though they were together for just a few days, it was long enough for Binsa to fall pregnant again and she regrets acting naively for a second time.

Once again, Binsa gave birth in Taplejung while the baby's father was absent. This time, the child was a girl, and thankfully no one expressed any disappointment. In a change of heart, Binsa's husband, which is how she now referred to him, recognized his responsibilities to his second family. He began sending them small amounts of money.

Understandably, Binsa still felt unsatisfied with the arrangement as she barely saw her husband and felt abandoned in remote Taplejung. The Maoist uprising was in full swing, and it seemed to her that everybody was joining them, though she felt scared of the insurgents herself. Neighbouring districts had witnessed massacres, and the violence was creeping closer. It was her idea to move to Pokhara, the largest city in western Nepal, to be closer to her husband so they could see each other more. He was now living back in his home district of Syangja, which neighbours Pokhara, with his first wife.

Binsa's husband agreed she should live in Pokhara, so he rented a room for them and paid all their living expenses. Just like her childhood, Binsa's relatively easy life resumed as her husband paid for everything, and there was no need for her to work. By now, her husband had four children with his first wife, and I can't help wondering where he found the money to support all his offspring. Government employees typically aren't paid all that well, although it is widely acknowledged that they may earn a lot from kickbacks and bribes. Sadly, corruption is rife across Nepal, and it is easier for most Nepalis to accept it rather than take on the challenge of stopping it.

Now that Binsa and her husband saw more of each other, their relationship changed. He became jealous and accused her of seeing other men behind his back. Though his accusations were baseless, he threatened to cut off his financial support for her and her children. Sensing that her position was vulnerable, Binsa wanted to protect herself by obtaining recognition that she was his wife. In particular, she sought legal acknowledgement that he was the father of her children. Consequently, she made the fateful decision to go to his home in Syangja and confront him and his first family, who had no idea that she existed.

When Binsa arrived at her husband's house, his first wife was away. A few days beforehand, his first wife's sister had died suddenly, and so his wife was visiting her *maiti ghar* (maternal home) for the death rites. When she returned and found Binsa in her home, there was a violent fight. Though the situation was the fault of their mutual husband, the two women took their anger out on each other, and he cowardly hid. Binsa's children were 6 and 3 years old by now, and they witnessed everything. Since Binsa refused to leave, she and her two children were confined to one room in the house and were eventually permitted to stay.

The two families lived together for an uneasy six months. Meanwhile, news of Binsa's appearance spread to her husband's mother, who lived alone in the family's ancestral home, situated another day's walk further into the hills. Given that life was so unbearable for everyone in her husband's house, at last, someone suggested that Binsa could live with her 'mother-in-law'. The old lady was lonely and was willing to have Binsa and her two grandchildren join her. Perhaps she was also wise enough to realize that all the hostility was of her son's making and that neither of the women were to blame. Though he permitted Binsa to live with his mother, from this point on, her husband no longer provided any money to support her and his children. He was furious with her for disturbing his quiet and respectable family life and she assumed he wanted to punish her for turning up at his house.

Over the next five years or so, life for Binsa and her children was relatively peaceful, but unfortunately, everything was about to change. When the first wife's oldest sons reached their late teens, they felt threatened by Binsa's son and believed he was after their father's land. Encouraged by their mother, they visited Binsa to beat her up and scare her off. They bludgeoned her over the head with a log and cracked her skull. As a result, she suffered significant brain injuries.

Binsa has no memory of what happened next. Her memory is blank.

Piecing together information from her family, it appears that she fled the house and wandered the streets for several years. When I asked what she ate while she lived on the street, she could not tell me. She roamed from place to place and was bedraggled and incoherent, an outcast whom others avoided. Perhaps it is a blessed relief that she is unable to recall what happened to her.

Binsa has only one memory from that time, and it is of the pain of giving birth. At some point, she was raped, perhaps it happened multiple times, but she does not remember those instances and has no idea who the man or men were. Instead, the agony of childbirth pierced through her blighted memory and seared itself in her mind. Once the baby girl had been born, her only recollection is of holding onto her tightly.

It is a miracle the baby survived, but praise God she did.

Binsa's next memory is of being in the small district hospital in Syangja with her baby, who was perhaps a few weeks old. She could not tell me who took her there, and she has never thanked them, though she would like to. Again, the memories are hazy, but she knows she gripped her daughter close to her while in the ward. Though she had lost her mind, as a mother, her instinct to keep and protect her child was always there.

With regular food and care, Binsa's mind began to heal, but she needed professional treatment. Staff from the hospital took her to the local police station, where a representative from Koshish was waiting to meet her. Koshish is the mental health self-help organization that WWR works with to this day (Koshish's work is described in the chapter about Tanya). The police gave Koshish's staff custody of Binsa, and they brought her and her baby daughter to the women's transit home they run in Kathmandu.

Binsa remained at the transit home for eighteen months. Thanks to their charitable work, she received medicine and counselling, which in time restored her sanity. Matrika, Koshish's founder, introduced me to her on my first visit to Koshish in January 2014. In most of the photos I took of her then, she looks well, but she stares vacantly into the distance in a few. In every shot, she clings tightly to her daughter, who was a toddler at the time.

A few months after I had met with her, Koshish considered her well enough to move to our Anugraha Ashram on the outskirts of the Kathmandu Valley. Among others, it was there that she met Maria, Hitu and later Somi. Though they treated her kindly and prayed for her, she gives particular credit to Esther and Nina for leading her to Christ. She has fond memories of the daily fellowship meetings she enjoyed at the home. Not long afterwards, she began attending church with

Hitu in Dhobighat, where Gyaneshwar Church had planted a congregation.

Wanting to know why she became a Christian, I asked her what made her believe and convert. She responded that she found great hope in the promise of eternal life. She knows Jesus has saved her, and now that she has won her peace of mind (which is why I have titled this chapter 'Winner'), she looks forward to a future life with Christ. She told me that the first thing she did each day was pray, and she recommended that others did likewise.

Nowadays, she does domestic work for the family of a local Christian man who owns a nearby school. She first took on the job when she lived at Anugraha Ashram, but when we relocated the women to a house nearer Kathmandu, she found her own accommodation and has been living independently ever since. WWR still supports her for rent and education costs, and Koshish provides her medicine, but otherwise, she is self-sufficient.

Back in Syangja, her two elder children continue to live and work. She speaks to them on the phone regularly, and they are in contact with their father, but Binsa and he do not speak. Both her son and daughter have got married, and she now has three grandchildren. Sadly, her son's wife left him, and he seems to be in a poor state, so she feels responsible for him.

Binsa's youngest daughter is now 9 years old, beautiful and intelligent. She is studying hard at school and has her own Christian faith. Understandably, she will, from time to time, ask who her father is. Binsa has not found a way to answer this question yet and will change the subject instead. I pray that it won't be long before she can respond appropriately to her daughter; otherwise, it could sour their close relationship if she continues to evade her daughter's questions.

As is the case for any child without a named father, Binsa's daughter does not have citizenship, and neither does Binsa herself. Binsa's parents have passed away, and she has lost touch with her siblings. Her greatest desire right now is to obtain citizenship for her daughter.

In April 2021 (after writing the chapter about Tanya), WWR began employing a lawyer to help our ladies with their citizenship cases. Our lawyer is a young female Christian, just 24 years old, and incredibly bright. She is methodically working to overcome all the barriers to citizenship that our women face. As I write this, our lawyer is about to accompany Tanya to Solukhumbu, where Tanya's birth family might have been traced. I find it hugely frustrating that Nepal's citizenship records are located separately in each district. For our ladies to make any progress, they must travel to their home districts, which is costly and time-consuming. I hope it won't be long before Nepal's government uses a computer system for its record-keeping that can be accessed from anywhere in the country. Given Nepal's mountainous terrain and arduous travel conditions, using modern technology would make a lot of sense.

In Binsa's case, it appears that she will need to make two trips. First off, she needs to go to Syangja to obtain a letter stating that she was not a citizen while living there and her husband did not recognize her. Following that visit, she needs to go back to Taplejung to where she was born and register her citizenship there. Hopefully, she'll be able to do this without losing too much time and money. Since her employer is a Christian, I hope she'll be able to take time off to make these journeys without losing her job.

I'm struck by Binsa's sense of satisfaction with her life. She is content with what she has and is proud of the transformation

God has worked in her. She knows full well that Christ won the victory for her, and she now counts herself as a winner. Esther tells me that she is popular among all our ladies, and I'm grateful that she can now bless others with her presence and peace of mind.

10

Tycoon: Anju

I have filled this book with my impressions of Nepal and its people, yet in the taxi to interview Anju, it was my turn to hear Saru's view of England. She was interested in seeing where my children lived at boarding school. She usually refers to their boarding houses as hostels, which I explained didn't quite describe them. So I pulled out my phone to show her photos of the old yet characterful country houses attached to the school where they live. She didn't seem all that impressed; Nepalis much prefer new things and will often leave cellophane wrapping or stickers on items for many months to give the impression they have just purchased them. In Kathmandu, old houses are left to fall apart or are torn down and replaced with new buildings; sadly, maintaining an old property is regarded as a waste of money. Despite being unimpressed with the buildings, Saru asked if the sloping roofs meant there was a lot of rain and snow, and she marvelled at the lack of dust in the photos. It fascinates me that she identified that so quickly.

It was certainly a dry, dusty day when we visited Anju. The sky was a yellow-grey hue, and as usual, we set off in a taxi, not knowing where we were going. We headed for a section of Kathmandu known as Pepsicola due to the large bottling plant in the area that produces Nepal's supply of Pepsi and Coke.

A wide dual-carriageway goes straight through the district and, relieved to be out of Kathmandu's more congested streets, cars and trucks speed up to make the most of the spacious road. Not on this day, though, as our taxi driver decided to crawl along, to and from the kerb, calling out to pedestrians for directions. Cars and trucks beeped at us, but our taxi driver ignored them all. Driving on Kathmandu's streets is frustrating enough, and it was awful knowing we were the cause of congestion. We were hunting for a large petrol station, not the most unique landmark, and after hollering at a few more pedestrians, we found it. Anju was there waiting for us.

I was eager to meet Anju. When Esther had visited her six months previously, with a painful foot, Anju had prayed for her, and Esther had been healed. Furthermore, Anju's husband had been a Christian – he had died of natural causes. After hearing so many stories of abusive men in the course of writing this book, I wanted to tell the story of a good husband. I became more intrigued to meet her when Saru and our driver called her for directions from the taxi. Anju's voice rang out clear and confidently through the mobile phone; if I was unaware of her circumstances, I would have assumed we were on our way to visit one of Nepal's elite.

Waiting for us at the side of the road was a small woman with a hunched back; some of her fingers were frozen in peculiar positions, and it was clear her arms didn't move the way they should. She looked to me to be at least 60 years old, but I soon realized she was the same age as me (mid-forties). In contrast to her immobility, her straight black hair was cut in a stylish bob. Almost all women in Nepal have long hair they wear tied up, so Anju looked unusually chic. Once we were sat opposite each other, I could see the confidence in her face that had been apparent earlier in her voice. I liked her immediately.

Born in Sindhupalchowk, Anju was the youngest of two daughters, and her sister is five years older than her. Her parents were farmers and owned a small strip of land that they cultivated. When Anju slipped away with friends to attend school for three days, her sister complained that she was left with all the housework. That was the end of Anju's schooling. However, she was a quick learner, and during her short attendance, she learnt the letters from Kha to Gya. This is like learning from A to Z, yet there are forty-nine characters in the Nepali alphabet, and she mastered all of them.

Anju is from the Magar ethnic group, and she had a devout Hindu upbringing. On a daily basis, her family worshipped Ganesh, a popular god with a human body and an elephant head. She describes Ganesh as an 'entry-level god'; everybody worships him, and only as someone becomes more devout do they begin to worship other gods. In her family's case, they also worshipped Bhagawati, a female goddess with great power who fought against the devil in favour of women. This goddess has spawned groups of feminist ascetics who live away from men. Though they remain Hindus, these women denounce the patriarchal dominance of men they say is not truly Hindu. As with any religion, Hinduism also has its factions and disagreements. At *Dashain*, Anju's family would sacrifice goats to appease Bhagawati. They also worshipped the male god Bhimsen, whom they feared because he has tremendous power.

Anju's parents owned three *aanas* of land; an *aana* is around the size of a single garage in the UK. Although they cultivated the ground as much as they were able, it was not big enough to support them. They also experienced tragedy while living there. Four children, two girls and two boys, born after Anju, died as babies. Her parents borrowed money against the land to pay for treatment, but in the end, they determined the land was 'bad luck' and decided to move elsewhere. When they eventually sold up and had paid off their debts, they only received 45 NRs for the property (30p nowadays – it's almost impossible to calculate what it was worth then, but certainly no more than £20). No one else wanted the ill-fated land.

At this point in our conversation, Anju's daughter Rupa, who had been sitting cross-legged next to her mum, got up. She prepared piquant lemongrass tea for Saru and me and an ayurvedic tea for her mother. We all appreciated the warm drinks; it was a cold day. The room was dark, and my back was positioned towards a draughty window. A cold breeze had been blowing down my neck since we arrived.

Having sipped our drinks and warmed up a little, Anju continued her story. She was 8 years old when the family moved nearer to the Tibetan border to another small patch of land they owned. It was a great move for her; the land was adjacent to the Araniko Highway, the main route between Kathmandu and Lhasa, the capital of Tibet. She enjoyed watching the handful of trucks go by each day between the two capitals. These days hundreds of trucks and buses use that road. It is dusty, dangerous, and features in the BBC documentary series *World's Most Dangerous Roads*. In the early 1980s, though, the road was barely used, and there were no buses at all. Given that both Nepal and Tibet/China favoured sealing themselves off from the world, it's easy to understand why the route to the border between them was so little used.

There was a glint in Anju's eye as she related the next part of her story. She proudly told me that she was clever and became a smuggler at 11 years old. The Aruniko Highway passes across the Friendship Bridge at the border between Nepal and Tibet. There are soldiers from both Nepal and China guarding the bridge, but they turned a blind eye to children, so she could cross and play on the bridge. She began taking goods to and fro across the bridge, earning 10 NRs for carrying 10m of cloth. On most days, she smuggled 100m across the border, so earnt 100 NRs. This was a substantial income, given that her family only received 45 NRs when they sold their land, and her older sister only earned 10 NRs per day.

The border region is exceptionally rugged, and there are countless overgrown mountain crevices and hideaways. When Anju became a teenager, she used the terrain to her advantage and earned more money by carrying greater quantities of goods and taking them by bus to Kathmandu. By the age of 17, she was a well-known smuggler and trader in the region. To our amazement, she details her wealth. She had 5 lakh (approx. £3,000) in the bank, which was kept under a friend's name as Anju didn't have citizenship at the time and so was unable to open a bank account herself. Thankfully, her friend was honest and didn't swindle the money from her. Anju also had 14 tolas of gold. A tola is equivalent to 11 grammes and, as a general rule of thumb, is worth 1 lakh (£600); therefore, her gold was worth around £8,400. Finally, there were the goods themselves, and at this point, she had 13 lakh (£7,800) invested in stock. Saru, Anju's daughter and I are astonished; Anju had accumulated this enormous wealth as an illiterate teenager in a remote region. She ought to be a star on the TV show *Dragon's Den*.

Unfortunately, Anju ran out of luck. All of her business activities had been carried out covertly, and she had not paid tax or import duties. One day, while travelling on a bus to Kathmandu with 13 lakh worth of stock, a policeman boarded the bus and demanded to see her papers. When she couldn't produce them, he confiscated everything. Thankfully she still had the money in her bank account and her gold, so she hadn't lost everything. She didn't know whether to laugh or cry.

While Anju had been busy making her fortune, her family had secured a marriage partner for her older sister. The two families had met, and the groom's family had presented them with *raksi* to seal the betrothal (this ceremony is described in Maria's story). However, Anju's sister had a boyfriend, an impoverished man who worked with their father and lived with them during busy seasons. Anju knew about the relationship and arranged for the couple to elope. She paid for all of the wedding accoutrements, such as a new blouse, sari, petticoat and earrings. She took the couple to Pashupatinath, the most sacred temple in Kathmandu. They married there, and Anju arranged accommodation for them in the capital.

Having left her sister and brother-in-law in Kathmandu, Anju went home to tell her parents about the marriage. When she gave them the news, her mother grabbed a stick and began to beat her. Mercifully, her father intervened and stopped the thrashing. However, the family still had an arrangement with the first groom's family. Not wanting to dishonour their name, Anju agreed to marry the boy herself, so the pact between the two families was not broken.

Anju's new home with her husband and in-laws was almost three hours from her roadside house. The route there took her up into the hills where it was cold and damp all year round; she had to stop her cross-border trading and become a dutiful daughter-in-law. At this time, Anju was highly religious. She had been brought up to believe in the *Swasthani Brata Katha*, an ancient Nepali Hindu text about the goddess Swasthani, who is chiefly known for protecting Nepal's king and queen. Despite venerating the acts of a female goddess, the text has been criticized in modern times for being highly sexist and patriarchal. Anju can still quote several mantras from the book, including the saying, 'If you look angrily at your husband you will become cross-eyed' and 'If a wife eats in secret, she will become a dog'. Anju believed all these and many more; she worked hard to adhere to them and wanted to be a perfect Hindu wife.

It wasn't until after her marriage that Anju began her period. She explained to us that her family was quite liberal. Rather than being banished to the cowshed, all she was required to do was stay away from male family members, avoid sunlight and stay at a relative's home. Those practices sound rather onerous and inconvenient to me, but Anju felt she could comply with them easily. Over half of Nepali women (let alone the men) believe that menstruation is the body's means of releasing impure blood, hence the need to evict menstruating women from ordinary life. Fifteen per cent of women across Nepal bury their menstrual pads rather than disposing of them with other household waste, believing the cloths to be unclean and impure. Anju was not allowed to cook and prepare food during her periods and was instead sent to work in the fields, which was more demanding than her usual chores.

Following ten months of relatively content marriage, the cold climate took a toll on Anju's husband, and he contracted tuberculosis. Anju and her brother-in-law took turns to carry him in a *doko* on their backs down the hill path to the main highway, where they caught a bus to Kathmandu. She still owned the 14 tolas of gold and had money in the bank. Over the next year, she brought him regularly to Kathmandu and paid for his treatment at the Tribhuvan University Teaching Hospital. Generally, he would be well for about three months and then relapse, so she would need to bring him to Kathmandu again.

Eventually, they decided it would be best if the two of them lived in Kathmandu so he could receive treatment more quickly and regularly. Anju had already given birth to her first daughter, but she was too busy caring for her husband to look after her daughter as well. Rather than bringing her with them to Kathmandu, she was left behind at her husband's home, where her grandparents could care for her. Her husband's family were not biased against girls, and they gave their grandchild buffalo and cow's milk, so she grew up healthy and strong.

Anju rented a flat for herself and her husband in Patan, but all her money had been spent on his treatment, so she took on low-paying work in a carpet factory. She proudly told me that it only took her three days to learn how to weave; again, she proved herself a savvy learner. Her husband was confined to their small room, but unusually for a Nepali man, he helped out with the cooking. At first, Anju's husband was oblivious to the numerous lakhs Anju had spent on trying to get him well, but when she took the job as a carpet weaver, he realized that she had used up her fortune on him. As a result, he trusted her completely and, from then on, followed her lead. He complied with everything she asked him to do.

Thankfully, Anju's husband's condition started to improve at around the same time she gave birth to their second daughter. With money Anju had saved from carpet weaving, they began a vegetable-selling business that they ran together under Anju's leadership. They leased a shop in Koteshwor, close to the busy junction I described in Lila's story. People and roads from all three cities in the Kathmandu Valley converge there. Though it is one of the most congested and dusty parts of the city, it is a fantastic location for any business.

Within four years, Anju had made her fortune again. The family's vegetable business owned three vehicles; two small trucks with canopies over their flatbeds and a larger truck. They employed farmers to cultivate around eighty-five *ropani* of leased land near Bhaktapur. A *ropani* is equal to sixteen *aanas*, and an *aana* is around the size of a large single garage, as mentioned earlier; their farmland amounted to eleven acres as far as I can tell, which undoubtedly must have produced a vast amount of vegetables. Now that they were financially secure, their elder daughter came to be with them, and the whole family lived in a modern rented house in Kathmandu. Their two daughters attended school and kindergarten, though Anju remained illiterate and performed all the calculations she needed to run her business in her head. In worldly terms, they had made it.

Tragically though, their good fortune was not to last. During the early 2000s, the Maoists were violently attempting to take control of Nepal. Though they were not yet active within the Kathmandu Valley, gangs called Y-cells (pronounced 'why-cells', short for youth-cells) were operating covertly in the valley. They terrorized local business owners, and when Anju mentioned them, Saru shuddered; she is clearly familiar with the fear they instilled. These unruly squads would beat up anyone they thought had money, under the pretext of funding the Maoists.

Early one morning, when Anju's husband was returning from a visit to their farm fields, a gang set upon him. They were after the cash he kept in a moneybelt on his waist. Having violently hit his face and broken his nose, they left him for dead in a ditch by the side of the road.

A local army patrol found him lying there and took him to their barracks in Chhauni, near the centre of Kathmandu. Since they suspected he was a Maoist, they gave him only very basic medical treatment. When he regained consciousness and explained that he was a shopkeeper, they still thought he was a Maoist. Eventually, Anju's husband asked them to bring him to their shop in Koteshwor, where he knew the local superintendent of police who would be able to vouch for him. Having proved his innocence, Anju's husband was free to leave army custody, but this was the beginning of another set of medical problems for him.

Four months later, Anju gave birth to their only son. Her husband was still suffering from ongoing nose and face pain. Eleven days after their son's birth, they conducted the traditional Hindu naming ritual, and Anju was pronounced ceremonially pure. The day was a celebration of new life, but the following morning, Anju awoke to discover that the right side of her body was paralyzed. She couldn't move, and she couldn't speak; understandably, it was terrifying for her. I cannot imagine how helpless she must have felt with two young daughters, a baby son, an injured husband and a business to run. It was devastating timing.

In typical Nepali fashion, her husband called everyone they knew to the house to gather their opinions on what should be done to help her. Unsurprisingly, the consensus was that she should go to a hospital, so she was lifted into a vehicle and taken to Patan Hospital. The doctor confirmed her paralysis but could not find a reason for it. After four or five days, she returned from the hospital as there was little they could do for her. She could speak a few words by this time but could not take herself to the toilet. As they were a wealthy family, they could afford someone to come and take care of her, but this wasn't to last.

Anju's family now pursued two courses of treatment for both her paralysis and her husband's injuries. They paid almost equal amounts of money for conventional medical treatment from the hospital and supplemented this with remedies prescribed by an expensive witchdoctor. The witchdoctor provided them with sacred threads he had prepared using incense and cow's urine. Cows are sacred to Hindus and are Nepal's national animal. If someone accidentally or intentionally kills one, they are tried as a traitor in Nepal's courts. We laugh at the thought of witchdoctors chasing cows down roads, where they roam freely in Nepal, trying to catch the urine coming out of them at just the right time. Each sacred thread they bought from the witchdoctor cost 28,000 NRs (approx. £180), and they tied them around their arms or ankles. During her periods, Anju was obliged to remove the thread. Before she could put it back on, the witchdoctor had to repurify it with more incense and cow's urine. It was an excellent money-earner for him. To afford their treatment, Anju and her husband began selling off all their assets to pay him and the hospital.

Anju's condition gradually improved; however, her husband's injuries troubled him. He always had drunk alcohol, but he became more reliant on it. He would socialize with other drinkers daily and eat at traditional Magar barbecue joints. His unhealthy lifestyle exacerbated his problems, and his nose did not heal. At significant cost, he was admitted to a private hospital in Jorpati, in the north-east of Kathmandu, where he spent fourteen months. At the end of this time, he was still unwell, and their money had run out, so the whole family returned to live in the hills with Anju's in-laws.

Two months later, Anju left her husband behind and returned with her children to Kathmandu. She was still mostly immobile but had just about got her life back on track when her father-in-law turned up with her husband. While staying with his parents, her husband had returned to his old drinking habits and had not taken care of his nose. He stank. His flesh had been eaten away, and there was a cavity between the bridge of his nose and the roof of his mouth. The rotten flesh that remained was putrid. Anju and her father-in-law took him to the

Teaching Hospital, where they diagnosed cancer. They removed the rotting flesh at the hospital, then sent him to a specialist cancer hospital in Bhaktapur, where he began chemotherapy. To afford this, the family took out a 24 lakh (£16,000) loan.

Since all of Anju's savings had been drained and they were destitute again, she moved her family to live at a *lokta* (traditional handmade paper) factory, where she also found a job. She managed to hold down her work there despite still not having complete mobility. She could not raise her hand above her elbow, and walking was extremely difficult for her.

Near the factory lived a man who had previously been a customer at their vegetable shop. He was a Christian, and Anju suspects that he had shared the gospel with her husband. Her husband had been keen to give church a try, but Anju had always said no. At one time, she had asked a Hindu priest about Jesus. He had told her Jesus was a blacksmith and therefore from an untouchable or Dalit caste. The priest also said that Jesus was hanged because he raped his own daughter. Given these lies, it's no surprise that Anju wanted to avoid Jesus at all costs. I wonder how many Nepalis have heard these same lies?

Knowing it would antagonize her, the Christian man did not share the gospel with Anju; instead, he showed love to her family by his actions. Church members would visit the family regularly to pray with them and help out with household chores. After doing this for some months, Anju's husband insisted that the family should go to church together. He told Anju that he expected to die, and if she remained unable to walk, there would be no one to look after their children: they had nothing to lose by going to church. Anju was adamant that she wanted to remain a Hindu, but she prayed one simple prayer on the way to church: 'God, if you are real, I need to see the truth today.'

Upon arriving at the church, they discovered the meeting was on the third floor. Anju had to be carried up the stairs by three people. She sat on a chair towards the back and continued to challenge God: 'If you're God, do something.' There was a visiting Filipino pastor who preached that day. When he said the words 'In Jesus' name', it seemed the whole congregation fell down in the Holy Spirit; yet still, Anju felt nothing. However, she sensed something good was going on. During worship, she found herself able to stand, and she decided to close her eyes like everyone else. Then, she felt someone touch her head, and she saw a vision of a man dressed all in white. His face was too bright to see. Her body felt immediately lighter, and miraculously she could raise her hand above her shoulder. Despite her initial scepticism, she became convinced that Jesus was real.

Before the Filipino pastor began his sermon, he asked the worshippers who had challenged God, and Anju immediately identified herself. She stood up to share her story with the entire congregation, and everyone was amazed at her transformation. At the end of the service, she walked down the stairs and experienced healing from all her paralysis from then on.

Anju's husband was astonished at her healing but was not cured himself; he became a Christian there and then, though. He philosophically told Anju that though she had been healed and he hadn't, he felt relieved that someone would be there to care for their children when he died. For the next few years, they lived together as a Christian family. Her husband gave up alcohol, and though they were poor, they enjoyed the help and fellowship of their new church. Both of them joined prayer groups and ministered to others. Anju found she had a gift for healing and witnessed many miracles as she prayed for others, including Esther's foot (as mentioned above).

In 2004, Anju was baptized with thirteen others in the Godawari River. Unfortunately, the water was contaminated, and she suffered from painful itching afterwards. God also performed another miracle in her life and supernaturally gave her the ability to read and write through a dream. When she awoke the following morning, she could easily read her Bible. Furthermore, she confidently showed me a hymn she wrote the day before my visit; it contained praise to God for healing her. The handwriting was ever so neat, and she credited God for that also. When God teaches someone to write, he also gifts them tidy handwriting.

Here is a translated version of Anju's hymn; some of the words and expressions are a little unusual, but it gives a vivid sense of her heart and love for Jesus:

When I was in swampy mud, Jesus found me.
Chorus: Very amazing, Jesus Christ's precious blood healed me.

I was stuck in the swamp; Jesus pulled me out.
Chorus

I was searching for my relatives; I found Jesus nearer than anyone else.
Chorus

Nails in hands, nails in feet; what a great mercy he did for me.
Chorus

He delivered a sinner like me, thanks to Jesus Christ, our King.
Chorus

Oh! Every day I will come and preach good news to all.
Chorus

I would rather die, but I will never leave you, Jesus.
Chorus

I will not get stuck in this world; Jesus' love is full in my heart.
Chorus

Five years after they became Christians, her husband passed away and just two months later, Anju gave birth to her youngest daughter. God had utterly healed Anju from her earlier paralysis, but in 2011 she was hit by a motorbike, and a heavy gate fell on her in a separate incident. These two events triggered a little of the earlier pain and resulted in some loss of mobility. Though she had her hands full with four children, she found time to help others and started a new business. She employed people with disabilities to carry out cross-border trading, as she had done as a teenager. Her involvement in the operation's day-to-day running ceased, but she encouraged them to do what they could, a great way to tackle life's challenges.

All of Anju's children are doing well at school; the eldest two have been baptized and have gone on to study for Master's degrees. The entire family attends church together, and they help out at the services. Her second daughter edits the church newsletter, which seems like a great way to honour the gift of literacy that God gave her mother. Anju has also paid off most of the 24 lakh loan she took for her husband's treatment and has just 3 lakh debt remaining. Evidently, she is still an extremely capable woman, and I love the combination of her deep love for Christ coupled with her energy and savviness.

Despite her hardships, she told me she was happy, and I truly believed her. The glint in her eye was there because she loves God and knows nothing is impossible with him. This is not the end of her story; her adventure with God is just beginning.

11

Blessed: Ishya

I hadn't slept well the night before interviewing Ishya. It was January 2022, and the Omicron variant of the coronavirus was sweeping the world. As cases surged in neighbouring India and hospitals became overwhelmed again, Nepal's government was wary of another outbreak and had ordered schools to close until the end of the month. This was devastating news for WWR's ladies, whose children had already missed months of their education. They are already disadvantaged compared to their peers who attend private schools, and now they faced several more weeks of online school if they could access it. Our ladies do not own computers and rarely have WiFi access. Their children would need to study via mobile phones on limited data plans. It was far from ideal, and I felt powerless to help them.

During the first lockdown in 2020, the 13-year-old son of one of the women we assist had given up on school altogether. He is the eldest of four children, and his father died several years ago in an accident at a construction site. Having observed his mother's plight, he decided to get a job to help her rather than continue with his tedious online lessons. It's hard to find fault with his reasoning, and his actions were admirable in many ways. Now, having found work as a mechanic and since the family had become reliant on his pay, he would probably never carry on with his education. Covid was impacting an entire generation of children; how many would miss out on their potential due to the disruption it caused?

Despite my heavy heart, it was delightful to see Saru again. As usual, we caught up with each other's news in the taxi on the way to the interview. My family and I had been trekking over the Christmas and New Year break, and I described our adventures above the snowline. At the highest point of our trip, the temperature had dropped below -10C, and I jokingly explained the perils of using a squat toilet at those temperatures. Nepali toilet etiquette requires rinsing the toilet and floor with water after use; however, the water had frozen, so there was a high chance of slipping over in the bathroom. We overcame this by using a trekking pole to steady ourselves while squatting, and Saru thought this was hilarious.

As we headed south of Kathmandu, several miles beyond the ring road, the congestion lessened, and small patches of green land appeared between the buildings. In the distance, we could see tall chimneys at the bottom of a river valley; these chimneys indicate the presence of brick kilns, and some were churning out black smoke. As usual, we had to ask for directions as we sought out the Pashupati Mandir in Godavari, where Ishya had agreed to meet us. We spotted her past the temple and jumped out of the taxi before walking with her to her home. Surrounding her room are workshops where Hindu temple ornaments are made. Some embellishments were small enough for the craftsmen to hold on their laps; however, one was larger than a bathtub. In this case, an artisan stood inside the decorative moulding to apply a gilt finish. Throughout my interview with Ishya, we could hear the ting-ting of hammers on metal coming from the workshops.

Ishya works as a labourer, and she had taken the day off so she could talk to us. Saturday is her regular day off to attend church, so she had offered to meet us in the middle of the week since her foreman would be angry if she took off two days in a row. She did not want to be accused of skiving off too often. Her co-workers are aware that she is a Christian. There is a common perception among Nepalis that people only convert to Christianity for money, so her workfellows mock her by asking why she's carrying such heavy loads and question why her church doesn't give her more support. She is always the last person to be paid during the many Hindu festival periods; her overseer tells her she doesn't need the money as she won't be celebrating. She endures these persistent low-level forms of persecution with grace.

Born in the western district of Rolpa in 1984, Ishya hails from the Magar caste, the largest indigenous ethnic group in Nepal. She is the eldest of five siblings, and her mother gave birth to four girls before a long-awaited son arrived. Once he was born, they decided the family was complete. Their household was exceptionally impoverished, and they survived by subsistence farming alone. Rice was too expensive for them, so they only ate it on special occasions. Most of the time, they ate *dhido*. Though many Nepalis regard *dhido* as comfort food, I find it hard to stomach. *Dhido* is made with just flour and water, and the bland mixture is stirred continuously as it cooks. Eventually, it coalesces to form a smooth thick paste that is served in one large lump. It resembles brown-grey dough and tastes no better than it looks. Having tried it a few times in traditional restaurants in more rural areas of Nepal, I feel no compunction about not trying it again.

As the eldest child, Ishya had to carry out much of the household work in their home. Sadly, she didn't have the opportunity to try school, but her younger siblings attended for a couple of years. When Ishya saw other children in her village heading off to school, she felt sad and was aware that she was missing out from a young age. Her family was Hindu, but they only performed *puja* for festivals and during solar or lunar eclipses. Even for Nepal, Rolpa is a poor area; none of her family went to a hospital or saw a doctor during their childhood. When her grandfather passed away at a relatively young age, there was no one to tell them why he had died. Despite their hardships, Ishya has always been healthy and strong, something she remains proud of to this day.

Ishya's childhood passed by fairly uneventfully, and it wasn't until she was 16 years old that her situation changed. Many of the teenagers in her village had already made the journey to Kathmandu to work at the capital's brick kilns, and her friends invited her to join them. An agent from the brick kiln was organizing a bus to take workers on the two-day journey from Rolpa to Kathmandu. He told her the work would be better than staying in the village. Ishya's parents were wary of the agent. Still, they did not stop her from leaving since they knew there were no opportunities for her in Rolpa. However, they did warn her to be careful since she was a girl.

Brick-making is an age-old manufacturing practice in Nepal. Most of Kathmandu Valley's temples and heritage buildings, which have been fortunate to survive the countless earthquakes that have struck the area, are constructed from traditional red bricks. Nowadays, good-quality bricks continue to be used for high-status buildings wishing to emulate the Newari (Kathmandu Valley) style; often, the bricks overlay a sturdy concrete interior. Alternatively, shoddy bricks that consist of little more than mud are used as a cheap building material if a family can't afford concrete. It was these cheap bricks that Ishya became involved in producing.

Approximately a hundred and ten brick kilns are thought to be operating in the Kathmandu Valley, and they contribute significantly to the poor air quality. During my research on the topic for this chapter, I found far more academic analyses of the impact of brick kilns on air quality than reports concerned with the working conditions of the labourers, which saddens me. Both issues are important and need to be addressed, but the working conditions that Ishya described to me are particularly abhorrent and deserve urgent attention.

Each working day began at 6 a.m. and lasted until dark; they had one hour off for lunch. Ishya was one of 150 workers at her particular brick kiln. The kiln overseer split the labourers into different groups, based on their ethnicity, to carry out the same task hour after hour, day after day. The work was incredibly repetitive, leading to injuries from constantly performing the same action. Since she was from Rolpa, Ishya's job was to lug unbaked bricks from where they were formed to the kiln. She carried sixteen bricks at a time; based on the standard brick weight for India, I calculate this would be a total weight of just over 40kg or 88lbs. She used a forehead *doko* strap, with no basket, to support the bricks on her back. Sometimes the distance between the brick stacks, where the mud bricks are dried before the firing process, was short, and at other times it was a long way to the kiln. No matter how far she had to carry them, her pay was the same. She earned 55 NRs (40p) per 1,000 bricks. Some days she might manage to carry this quantity; on others, she could not complete her quota. At the end of the month, the workers received their pay; however, the kiln managers always subtracted money from the workers' wages to cover the cost of the food they provided communally. At night, the labourers slept under zinc sheets propped over the piles of bricks. I'm sure they must have been constantly exhausted and would have had no energy left to appeal for better working conditions.

Ishya worked like this for a year, and during that time, had no days off. On Saturdays, the workers were given the afternoon off to bathe and visit the local shops. Given their low pay, Ishya could only afford soap to wash herself and the occasional cheap item of clothing to replace the few she wore until they were falling off her. She was unable to save a single rupee and could not send any money to her family as she had hoped. Yet, she remains positive about her experience and miraculously counts her blessings. She told me that at least she had rice to eat there rather than *dhido*, so it was better than life in Rolpa. Throughout my own life, I have never considered rice to be a luxury and yet here she was modelling such grace and humility about the desperate situation she endured. I felt stunned and strangely disgusted with my own attitude to life and lack of appreciation for everything I have.

Despite my admiration for her contentment, I couldn't help wondering if this attitude allows the brick kilns to continue operating. If the workers believe they have no right to staple foods and safe living conditions, they will continue to be exploited. While brick kilns within Lalitpur (Patan), where Ishya worked, must be licensed, they continue to employ child labourers and do not provide adequate safety equipment. A survey[9] of brick kiln workers found that only 42 per cent knew child labour was illegal. Shockingly, just 2 per cent knew about minimum wage legislation. I told Ishya that I would love it if someone reading her story took action to enforce safety rules at brick kilns, and she was delighted with this idea.

Not every aspect of Ishya's life was controlled by the kiln bosses. While there, she fell in love with another worker from Rolpa. She admired his hard work, and when I enquired if he was handsome, she said he looked like her. I think she meant that he was from the same ethnic group!

The two of them returned to Rolpa to marry, but neither of their families were happy. Though her parents didn't object to the marriage, they reminded her that they had warned her to keep away from men. Their desire had been for her to return with money, not a man. His parents were much more upset by the relationship as they had already begun arranging a marriage for him with a girl from their village. Nevertheless, neither family felt it necessary to stop the wedding. Having accepted the traditional *tika* blessing from her in-laws, Ishya went to live with her new husband at his family home, three hours from her *maiti ghar*.

After spending six months in Rolpa, Ishya and her husband returned to work at the same brick kiln in Kathmandu they had recently left. They felt they had no choice, and at least they would be together. It wasn't long afterwards that Ishya discovered she was pregnant; when she missed her period, a pregnancy test at Patan Hospital confirmed the news. Her caring husband insisted on an ultrasound a few weeks later to check on the baby's health, which was good. Ishya continued to work at the brick kiln until the eighth month of her pregnancy; though the brick kiln manager knew she was expecting, he made no concessions for her.

Heavily pregnant, Ishya and her husband made the long journey back to Rolpa by bus and returned to live with his parents again. Ishya took on the tasks of a traditional daughter-in-law and did most of the domestic work, despite her condition. Her husband resumed his previous way of life and became a subsistence farmer again. His elder brothers had already left the family home, so his parents were on their own and should have been glad of the company and help around the house; however, they remained indifferent to Ishya.

When it came time for Ishya to give birth, her mother-in-law helped her deliver in the couple's room. The labour went relatively smoothly, and she gave birth to a beautiful baby girl. However, her mother-in-law offered no further assistance once the girl was born. The following day, Ishya had to wash her soiled clothes, rinse the bloodstained bedding, clean up the room and care for her new daughter. I asked Ishya if perhaps her mother-in-law might have shown more compassion towards her if she had given birth to a boy, but she thought not. Ishya had scuppered the family's plans for their son to marry into another family from the village, and they continued to hold that against her.

Another year passed in the family home, and Ishya gave birth to a second daughter in 2004. The treatment she received from her in-laws wasn't great throughout this period, but neither was it terrible. She is grateful that they provided her with the same food they ate, which helped her maintain her excellent strength and give birth to healthy daughters. In fact, Ishya's health was so good that she and her husband decided to return to the brick kiln shortly after the birth of her second daughter.

Ishya's health was not the only reason they wanted to return to Kathmandu; there was also a significant push factor: the Maoist uprising. Rolpa is the birthplace of the Maoist movement in Nepal and, since 1991, had elected communist politicians to the parliament. In 1996, Maoists had attacked a police post in Holeri, Rolpa and declared war. The rebel forces had soon displaced the district government and taken absolute control. It became home to the Maoist's political and military leadership, who used the area to model what they were trying to achieve. The Maoists built roads, dispensed justice and consolidated power. Though the insurgents had some lofty ideals, in practice, they ruled by force and intimidation; local residents were caught in the battle between them and the state.

Ishya knows many people that died on either side of the war. She told me that both the Maoists and police would turn up at their home and demand loyalty. On many occasions, they were forced to turn up at rallies to give the appearance that the Maoists had popular support. At other times, the police or army would show up and threaten to shoot them if they gave food or shelter to the Maoists. Her family tried to remain out of the conflict and wanted to live in peace, but it became harder and harder to remain neutral. As a result of all this unrest, Ishya and her young family returned to live and work at the brick kiln. Their story is like so many others. During the Maoist uprising, the population of Kathmandu soared as vast numbers of people fled from rural areas to the relative safety of the capital. In 1991, 1 million people lived in the valley, yet by 2011 there were 2.5 million residents.

Once the family had resettled at the brick kiln, Ishya's main task was to keep her children out of harm's way. She wasn't employed directly by the kiln owners, but she tried to be helpful and earn a little on the side. Her husband received a small promotion; he now joined a gang of workers accompanying the kiln's trucks. When they reached construction sites, he would help unload soil from the truck to build up foundations. Loose soil is a common building need in Nepal, where many structures are erected on slopes, and sites have to be levelled off.

As her two girls grew older, they attended a low-cost government school. Ishya gave birth to a son in 2009, and this time she went to the government hospital in Thapathali for delivery. She describes her labour as taking place in luxury since she received both medicine and care. Everything was going well for them. Her husband received a second promotion, and he now drove trucks to and from the kiln with deliveries. His success meant the family could afford to rent a room near the brick kiln, and they no longer had to sleep under zinc sheets with the other labourers. Sadly, though, tragedy was just around the corner.

When their son was just 4 years old, Ishya's husband was on his own at a steep hill. He had taken the truck there to collect mud and was shovelling it out of the hillside onto the back of the vehicle. As he dug deeper into the hill, he disturbed the earth around him. Eventually, the mud tunnel he had formed collapsed around him. The soil buried him, and both filled and crushed his lungs. Rescuers appeared, who dug him out of the mudslide. But though he was still breathing when they reached him, tragically, he died on the way to the hospital.

Workers from the brick kiln came to Ishya with the awful news, and she was naturally in shock. She never saw the place where her husband died, and neither did she attend his funeral at Pashupatinath Temple. The brick kiln covered the funeral costs, and male workers were permitted to aid the cremation. Pashupatinath is the most sacred temple in Kathmandu, and the complex is home to many *sadhus*, older men who renounce worldly life. I have only visited twice, and it is an extremely dark spiritual place. The temple is alongside the Bagmati River, which flows from there through Kathmandu, where the city's residents use the river as a rubbish dump, and south to India, where it joins the Ganges. Every devout Hindu hopes that by having their ashes scattered in one of these sacred rivers their soul will join with the goddess Ganga.

Apart from paying for her husband's funeral, the management at the brick kiln did not offer Ishya any further compensation, despite having caused her husband's death by not providing safety equipment. The only silver lining in all of this was that, unlike many of the women WWR supports, her husband's death was sudden, so Ishya had not gone into debt trying to cure him of an illness. Many of our ladies have taken out huge loans trying to treat their husbands so that by the time they pass away, they have not only lost the family's breadwinner but have loan sharks harassing them. Ishya was left with three children and no money when her husband died, but she did not owe money to anyone.

For the remainder of the month, Ishya felt numb and could barely function. Her children kept her going, and at the start of the following month, she realized that she needed to work if she had any hope of paying her rent. There was no way she wanted to end up homeless. Ishya visited nearby construction sites and offered her skills as a labourer. She felt qualified to do nothing else. Although some people call her names and accuse her of promiscuity just because she has to talk to men to carry out her job, she has worked as a casual labourer ever since.

Many months later, a man at the construction site told her that if she wanted food for her children, she should try going to a church because they handed out supplies. He was a Christian and knew that his church would be generous towards her. Ishya was so desperate that, although she had no interest in converting, she gave church a try. Once at the church, she discovered that she enjoyed the service and left feeling better than when she arrived.

The next part of her story is somewhat controversial for us at WWR. As part of its ministry to the vulnerable, the church ran a hostel and school. In many ways, it was not all that different from an orphanage, and they encouraged foreign sponsorship. There is an entrenched belief in Nepal that some children are better off away from their impoverished parents. This is not WWR's view, and we believe it is far better to keep families together. However, we also believe in encouraging the women we help to make informed choices to empower them. Sadly, some extremely corrupt orphanage owners traffick children and prey on the kindness of foreign donors to make money from their sympathy. We have no evidence to suggest this is the case with the church hostel, but it is important to remain vigilant. For more on this issue, please read *Little Princes* by Conor Grennan and learn more by visiting the website of Next Generation Nepal, the NGO he established to reunite families (see 'How to Help' section).

Upon discovering church-run hostels for both boys and girls that might be willing to feed, clothe and educate her children for free, Ishya was desperate to enrol them. She approached the pastor's wife, who gave her some sound advice. First, she was told that children in the hostels would be raised as Christians; Ishya needed to become a Christian herself. This was not to put overt pressure on Ishya to falsely convert but was done in the family's best interests. The pastor's wife knew the family had a better chance of remaining intact if they shared beliefs.

Secondly, there was a formal process to go through, and Ishya would need the correct paperwork before they could join up. I was relieved to hear this, as it demonstrates to me that the church was doing its best to avoid encouraging the trafficking of children; they only helped those in genuine need. As a result, Ishya returned to Rolpa to obtain her children's birth certificates, her husband's death certificate and her citizenship. She made the journey as soon as she could afford to. Lastly, the pastor's wife advised against enrolling all three of her children but suggested keeping her eldest daughter with her for company and friendship. Ishya appreciated the sense of this; her meagre wages could afford food, clothing and school classes for one child.

After six months of preparation, Ishya's two youngest children joined the hostels and have thrived since being there. She sees them every Saturday at church, and during the lockdowns in 2020 and 2021, they came to live with her. I trust that God is leading the church elders in Nepal; I pray God will oversee their hostels and guard against any form of exploitation or abuse. My children are at boarding school in a different country, so I'm not in a position to judge anyone; however, in my opinion, if this church could have helped pay Ishya's food bills and contributed to her children's education without requiring the family to separate, that may have been better. In Ishya's case, the hostels helped meet a vital need at a critical moment. Before enrolling her children, she admitted to contemplating suicide.

When Ishya compared her previous life with her new Christian life, she told me it was like comparing heaven to hell; the change is so profound. Two years after joining the church, she was baptized in the Godavari River. At about the same time, WWR began supporting her, for which she is extremely grateful. She cherishes God's love for her, feels enormously blessed, and her faith is strong. When she prays, God answers.

There remains one thorn in her side. Her husband's older brother also migrated from Rolpa to Kathmandu to work in a brick kiln when he was a teenager. He lives nearby and is adamant that she should give up on Christianity once her children have completed their education through the church. Of course, she plans to defy him, but it will be difficult for her.

Nowadays, her eldest daughter still lives with her and aspires to work in a bank. Her second daughter loves to worship and plays the piano at church. They are keen to be baptized at the same time and are waiting until the youngest has their pastor's approval. I'm pleased her girls want to go through baptism together as it indicates they remain close. Like young boys worldwide, Ishya's son wants to become a footballer.

Before Saru and I left, Ishya was keen to show us all the gifts she had received from WWR over the years; she had looked after everything we have ever given her, and I was amazed at their good condition. She is so thankful to her sponsors, who I hope are reading this. In every corner of the room there was a gift; she showed us a cooking pot, the carpet, a duvet, the fleece she was wearing, a shawl and a *kurta*. On top of one pile was a bag containing toiletries that one of the wives from the British Camp generously gifted to our ladies. She listed the luxuries such as shampoo and lip balm she had enjoyed since she received it.

On our way out of her building, she told us about her Christian landlord, who ignored all the local gossip that she was immoral for talking to men at work, and offered her a room. His kindness has enabled her to host church fellowship meetings in her room. I asked what she prayed for, and she revealed that her heart was for other single women; she longs for Nepali society to look on them with favour. I pray this too; she is a beautiful model of God's kindness and compassion at work. I love that there are many Christians involved in her story, and together we have been able to usher her family into the kingdom of God, where she has discovered so many blessings.

12

Runners: Ema and Riya

Despite its size and population, Kathmandu stills feels like one sprawling village. Over the past month, I had begun to notice gangs of boys out on the streets during the day. With the schools still closed due to Covid, they were understandably bored, and so they roamed about in the streets trying to keep warm and occupied. These gangs may seem rather ominous to anyone who doesn't know Kathmandu. Yet, in Nepal, children generally respect their elders. As the boys wandered about, I noticed shopkeepers engaging with them in friendly banter; no one shooed them away. I love that Kathmandu is one of the safest capitals in the world, and everyone talks to everyone else, just like a village.

Since this was my final interview, meeting Saru for the last time outside Ekta Books was bittersweet. However, it was our first time to take a taxi together to the west of the city since only a few of the ladies WWR supports live in this area. While in the taxi, we chatted about Nina, WWR's second-in-command, who is married to Saru's cousin. Along with all of the residents of our women's home, Nina had been sick with Covid over the previous few weeks. Saru had caught up with Nina by phone the previous evening, and we were both relieved that she was almost fully recovered. Nina lives with her mother-in-law, Saru's aunt, who is in her sixties and had been especially poorly, but mercifully, she too was now recovered. Thankfully Omicron was proving to be much milder than previous coronavirus variants.

Saru and I got out of our taxi in front of the imposing Vayodha private hospital; Ema ran over to greet us, and we followed her to her home. Initially, we had to cross a decrepit brick and plank bridge over the Balkhu River. Ema believed it was more than one hundred years old, and by the looks of it, that may be true; it certainly wasn't recently constructed. We carefully stepped from plank to plank to avoid falling through the gaps in the bricks, and made it safely to the other side.

Ema lives on the grounds of Revival Baptist Church. The church rents perhaps an acre of uneven land and as well as building a church hall, has also erected large single rooms to house vulnerable families. The pastor's family lived on the grounds too, and everyone shared a couple of simple toilets in an outhouse. I had visited about five years before when the buildings were new, and though they were basic, they seemed adequate. However, having been constructed from cheap bricks and tin roofs, I was sad to see they had not weathered well. The compound appeared unkempt and dilapidated; apparently, the church was looking for a new piece of land, and maybe that was why they had stopped maintaining their current buildings.

Despite outside appearances, Ema's room was colourful and tidy. Hanging from the centre of the ceiling was a paper lantern created from tens of multicoloured pieces of paper. It was stunning, and Ema told us her daughter, Riya, had made it. Saru and I settled on the wooden couch, and since it was only 9 a.m., it was still cold enough to see our breath. Ema warmed us up with cups of milky tea, and her pastor joined us to pray. He was delightful, but I sensed he wanted to know what was going on and why I was there. As it turned out, he was overjoyed that I was recording the stories of Christian women.

He was so enthusiastic that, at one point, it didn't appear that he would leave us to talk! I prefer to interview the women privately to protect any secrets they may share. Although he was Ema's pastor, I know many of our women don't reveal every detail of their personal histories to their church ministers and I didn't want to assume that Ema was happy to talk in front of him. I was thankful when he got up to go, and we were free to talk openly.

Ema was born in 1979 in a small village near Mechinagar in the far eastern district of Jhapa; the border with India was just a few miles away. She was one of ten siblings, of which there were four boys and six girls, and she was the eldest daughter. Though her parents owned the house where they lived, there was no land to farm. Instead, her parents collected firewood to sell at the roadside or local bazaar.

Ema's mother sounds like a remarkable and rather eccentric woman. She must have been pregnant for most of Ema's childhood, but she never told the family when she was expecting a baby (perhaps she didn't know herself). One day, Ema remembered her mother coming home from cutting grass with a newborn baby. There was no prior warning; the baby was simply there that evening. On other occasions, her mother would be late to prepare the evening meal, so Ema and her siblings would go and look for her. They would discover their mother somewhere, having just given birth and holding a new baby. It was a family joke, and Ema giggled as she told us about all the surprise babies that kept on appearing. Remarkably, only one of Ema's brothers died in childhood, meaning that despite their poverty, her family beat the odds for child mortality.

Ema's first memory is from when she was around the age of 7. Her eldest brother, who was 14 years old, disappeared one day. His loss was keenly felt by the family because he was the only child they had allowed to attend school. Thanks to relatives who already lived there, they discovered he had gone to Nagaland. This Indian state borders Myanmar, and he would have travelled about 300 miles from Jhapa to reach it, passing between Bangladesh and Bhutan and through Assam. Nagaland is famed for its headhunting tribes and has a reputation for fearsome warriors. Though firmly part of India today, the Naga tribes did not give up their independence easily. The state had been home to fierce rebellions against both British India and independent India after partition.

Soon after her brother's departure, Ema's father became sick and began to suffer from a painfully swollen stomach. To pay for his treatment, the family took a loan from a moneylender for 7,000 NRs (around £50) and put up their only asset, their house, as equity. They had to move out of their home and began renting a room in Pathari, Sunsari, two districts west of Jhapa. They continued to collect and sell firewood to make ends meet.

The family's new house was along the east–west highway, which runs the length of the Terai, parallel to Nepal's border with India. Less than two weeks after Ema's mother had given birth to her tenth child, a baby girl, she and Ema's father were pushing a cart loaded with around twenty bundles of firewood along the road. A speeding car came from the opposite direction and hurtled into them. The driver, an Indian businessman, was drunk and the accident left Ema's father critically injured. Thankfully, the driver took responsibility for the accident and got Ema's father to a hospital, where he paid for his treatment.

Every day for the next month, Ema and her mother travelled half an hour by bus to visit her father at the Ghopa Hospital in Dharan. Tragically, his injuries were severe, and he died despite the best efforts of the doctors and nurses. The Indian businessman did not abandon the family, though, and covered the funeral costs; he also gave them 50,000 NRs (£350) with which they bought a paddyfield. Ema's mother was now a single mother with nine children relying on her, but the purchase gave them some security.

Ema hails from a high-caste Chettri family, and her mother was a strict Hindu. Every day she insisted that the family perform *puja* to Shiva, god of death, in their house. However, Ema did not understand who or what she was worshipping. It was essential to her mother that the funeral rites for Ema's father were carried out correctly. Usually, a man's oldest son would prepare the body for cremation and accompany it to the *ghats*, level platforms alongside rivers where bodies are laid out before being set alight. Since her brother had left, and the funeral had to occur immediately, these tasks fell to Ema's uncle. Her brother turned up a week or so later to comfort his mother. He brought a Bible with him that none of the family recognized nor could read. When he returned to Nagaland, he left it with them.

Another aspect of Hinduism that was important to Ema's mother was ensuring that Ema followed the correct rituals when she began menstruating. When her first period arrived at age 14, Ema was sent to a relative's house, where she was kept away from men and sunlight. During her subsequent periods, Ema was not allowed in their kitchen nor to perform *puja*. We laughed at this because Ema couldn't remember her mother following these rules; we wondered if her mother ever had a period, given that she was constantly pregnant.

Ema was now considered an adult, and consequently, she was deemed old enough to leave the family home and find work. Her mother sent her to live with one of her brothers. Traditionally, an older uncle is called Mama, which for us is a somewhat confusing name for a man; and his home is referred to as *Mama ghar*. Ema referred to her uncle's wife as Maiju. This couple lived in Itahari, the largest town in Sunsari, where they owned a shoe shop in the heart of the bazaar. All told, there were eighteen family members in their household and four staff from the shoe shop. It was Ema's job to cook and clean for every one of them; on occasion, Maiju would help, but most of the time, all the work fell to Ema. Unsurprisingly, she said she often felt exhausted.

Although Ema didn't receive any money for her efforts, the food was good in Itahari, and the family gave her some clothes. Once a year at *Dashain*, she was given a small sum to cover the bus fare to see her mother. Whatever change she had from this, usually just 50 or 60 NRs (30p or 40p), she gave to her mother to help provide for her younger siblings. Though Mama suggested she go to school and learn to read and write, Maiju would not allow this, so she remained illiterate.

While living in Itahari, Ema became more devout in her Hindu faith. Her *Mama ghar* participated in Hindu rituals at Itahari's many temples, and Ema enjoyed the atmosphere of these. Since she was just a teenager, she relished the chance to dress up in some borrowed finery for the events. The attention she received when given *tika* blessings from her relatives was also to her liking. As a result, when Ema's mother became a Christian and threw out the family's idols, Ema was very angry with her.

Ema's mother had become sick; she was fatigued all the time and barely ate. Ema's eldest brother had been visiting his mother every couple of years. He told her that the Bible he'd left in their home was medicine. None of the remaining family members could read the Bible, but they kept it in their home on a shelf. One night, Ema's mother was in particular distress and, willing to try anything, decided to place the

Bible/medicine under her pillow as she slept. That night she heard a kind and trustworthy voice telling her to throw out her idols. When she woke up, she felt healthy and strong; her sickness had gone. She gathered up all the pictures and statues of Shiva in their home and threw them into the cesspit under their toilet. She knew that Christian pastors could explain the Bible, so she went directly to a church, found a pastor and told him she wanted to be baptized.

When Ema saw her mother soon after this, her mother excitedly told her what had happened and shared the gospel with her. Ema was unconvinced; however, at the age of 20, Ema experienced the gospel for herself. Tired of working endlessly for her Mama and Maiju, she went to Nagaland to spend six months with her older brother. Astonishingly Nagaland is home to one of the most vibrant Christian communities in the world. These remote hills, formerly home to ruthless headhunters who proudly displayed the skulls of those they had killed as decorations on their homes, is now 90 per cent Christian.

American Baptist missionaries first arrived in Nagaland in the 1830s. However, they were repeatedly driven away by the tribespeople, who did not want to welcome outsiders. On occasion, the missionaries were also caught up in unrest caused by fighting between the British, who ruled India at this time, and the tribes. It wasn't until the 1880s that the missionaries established a permanent and continuous presence in Nagaland that allowed them to disperse evangelists across the region. Initially, they built schools and helped to write the first Naga alphabet. In the 1890s, they began medical work and demonstrated the love of Christ in practical ways. Their strategy was successful, and vast numbers of Nagas converted to Christianity. Since the American Baptists had trained local evangelists and allowed them to lead the church, when the Americans (along with all foreigners) were thrown out of India following independence in 1947, the church continued to grow.

In the 1950s, Catholic missionaries joined the quest to convert the headhunting tribes, and they too had enormous success, setting up countless schools and hospitals. At the same time, missionaries from elsewhere in India came to Nagaland. These native missionaries brought a Pentecostal form of Christianity with them that incorporated indigenous drums and dancing. Their focus during church services was more spiritual and charismatic than either the Baptist or Catholic forms of Christianity that the Nagas had so far experienced. Many dramatic healings took place, and consequently, a revival of Christian faith swept the state. The churches set up by these indigenous missionaries became known as revival congregations. The church Ema is part of in Kathmandu is a 'Revival Baptist'; her pastor converted to Christianity in India, hence the name and affiliation.

Nowadays, the statistics are astonishing; more than 90 per cent of Nagaland's around 2 million population identify as Christian, and of those, 75 per cent are Baptists.[10] Consequently, Nagaland has more Baptists than any US state, including Mississippi or Alabama, referred to as the 'Bible Belt' in the US. The state has a Christian council and is just one of three majority Christian Indian states.

I doubt Ema knew any of this when she went to Nagaland to visit her brother. He was now a member of one of the revival churches. While with him, she contracted malaria, which was unfortunately prevalent in the area. Regrettably, deaths due to malaria were commonplace. She remained at her brother's home and refused to go to the hospital. The general view was that if you went to a hospital with malaria, you wouldn't come out again (the same sentiment is expressed nowadays in Kathmandu regarding coronavirus).

Ema was very sick and very scared. Members of her brother's church prayed for her and taught her from the Bible. Given her mother's recent testimony, she was now willing to give the gospel a hearing. One night, she, too, heard voices; however, these voices were hostile and threatening. The Hindu goddesses Saraswati and Laxmi appeared to her and began to lambast her: 'Are you leaving us?', 'You are going to the way of truth' and 'We'll make you sick'. Rather than frightening her away from Christianity, she chose to believe in the gospel, which was her turning point. The following day, she signed up for one week of Bible classes at the church; she still couldn't read but listened to everything they said. Immediately after that, she decided to be baptized.

The night before her baptism, a demon came to her in a dream and tried to bury her. Though she didn't feel as if she knew how to pray, she cried out to God: 'Please, Father, rescue me, I want to be baptized.' Following this, she had a good night's sleep and woke up feeling at peace. The next day she was baptized, along with fourteen others, in a stream, and afterwards, the church held a boisterous party for them. Given that Nagaland is a Christian state, no secrecy was required.

Ema was now a Christian, and having returned to her family in Nepal, she needed to find work. A distant male relation told her he could fix her up with a job in Kathmandu, so along with her younger sister, the three of them set out for the capital.

Soon after arriving in Kathmandu, her relative took her to the home of an Indian man. The three entered a pair of large black gates, and Ema and her sister hung back while her relative spoke with the Indian man. The two women eavesdropped on the conversation and heard the Indian man describe the two of them as beautiful. Immediately, Ema was alert. Having lived in the bazaar in Itahari, she was street smart. She had heard tales of women trafficked to Indian brothels from Kathmandu.

Ema and her sister backed out of the gates without being noticed; once in the street, they waited for their relative to come out. When he appeared, they told him they knew what he was up to, and they could not be intimidated or coerced. They demanded that he take them straight to a police station or a church. Wanting to avoid getting into trouble with the police, he chose to take them to a church.

The two girls ended up at nearby Putalisadak Church, and their relative disappeared. A helpful deacon was in the church hall, and he invited the girls to live at his home temporarily; they would help out with household chores in exchange for board and lodging. This arrangement lasted for a month before Ema decided to move to a Christian hostel. The arrangement at the hostel was similar, board and lodging in exchange for domestic work, but the hostel supervisors gave her a small amount of cash as well. The pay was just 1,200 NRs (£8) per month, which was not enough to allow her to send anything back to her mother, so after two months, she moved on again.

This time, Ema rented a private room and found work at a garment factory where the workers made clothing for export. She was paid a piecemeal rate for each item she completed. The raw materials came from India, and the agent responsible for sourcing them regularly visited the factory from Delhi. This man was originally a Nepali Magar from Pokhara, and he quickly noticed Ema and began flirting with her. Upon discovering she was a Christian, he told her he was a believer too, and Ema thought all her dreams had come true. She was smitten.

Having known each other for only four or five days, the man proposed, and shortly after, Ema set out for Delhi with him on the bus. They didn't have a wedding ceremony but now referred to each other as husband and wife. She moved into his room in Delhi, and sadly the situation quickly turned sour. Ema had brought her Bible with her and prayed regularly, expecting her new husband to join in. He revealed that he was not a Christian and had lied to her because he liked the look of her. She had noticed a thread around his wrist and chosen to ignore it, but she realized she had been naïve; the thread indicated his dedication to Hindu gods.

Their relationship became abusive. Ema's husband did not allow her to work, and neither did he trust her; while he was at the office, he locked her in their room. On his return, if he noticed her Bible or hymn book, he would rip out the pages she was reading from. Eventually, he began to take his anger out on her directly, and he beat her. Understandably, she became desperate to leave. Thankfully, her theology was sound, and she knew God would forgive her for marrying him; she just had to get away.

The two of them managed a year together in Delhi, and during that time, Ema became pregnant. She started to plan her escape from him and knew she would have a far better chance of getting away from him in Kathmandu rather than Delhi, where she knew no one. She hoped to persuade her husband that they would be better off living in Kathmandu; it was too hot for her in Delhi, and there were relatives in Kathmandu who would help her with the baby when it arrived.

Ema's arguments worked on her husband, and the two of them returned to Kathmandu. They lived together for another year, and both worked at the garment factory until their baby girl, Riya, was born. Ema gave birth to her alone at the maternity hospital in Thapathali since her husband refused to come with her. She remained with him, though, and after the birth, they set up a small vegetable stall that Ema could manage while tending to baby Riya. However, the beatings continued, and Ema still hoped to get away from him; she was just waiting for the right opportunity.

Eventually, Ema could endure her husband and his thrashings no longer. Riya was 2 years old, so she took her and what belongings she could carry to her sister's house for a week. They hid out there, expecting her husband to pound on the door looking for them at any moment, but he didn't. In the end, Ema stole back to their room in the middle of the day, when she hoped he would be at work, and discovered he had packed up his belongings and left as well. She has never seen him again.

Since then, Ema has done household work and provided everything for Riya herself. The two of them have always attended church together, and both have a strong faith. At this point, we were joined in Ema's room by her pastor's wife, who we discovered is her actual sister. Nepali women refer to each other as Baini (younger sister) and Didi (older sister), no matter if they are real sisters or not. However, these two are genuinely sisters. I told Ema's sister that we had enjoyed hearing about their mother and all the unusual places she unexpectedly gave birth. Ema revealed that she was born in a paddyfield, and her sister told us her birthplace was a wheat field. We all laughed at this before catching up on some family news. Their mother is still alive and living in Sunsari. Their eldest brother returned from Nagaland and pastors a Baptist church in Morang (between Sunsari and Jhapa). Riya is in the first year of a four-year Bible college course, and Ema is so proud of her. The revival churches permit full equality for men and women, so Riya can try her hand at everything. She helps out with youth ministry, leads worship and preaches. I asked if women could become pastors and was told that they could.

I wanted to end this book with a focus on the next generation of Christian women, and so Saru and I headed off to meet with Riya to find out what's next for Nepal's women. Thankfully we found a taxi quickly; the city had introduced odd–even restrictions on number plates to curb the spread of Covid. Only those vehicles with even numbers could drive on even-numbered calendar days and vice versa. The taxi took us around the ring road, and we headed out on the radial road that leads to Hattiban.

Riya is now 21 years old and was waiting by the roadside to meet us. We sat down in a nearby café to chat, and she excitedly told us all about her life. We broke the ice by asking if she too knew about her incredible grandmother who gave birth in unexpected places; she had heard the stories as well! It's as if their family matriarch has become a folk hero for her exploits in pregnancy and childbirth.

Riya has no memory of her father, and her earliest memories are of frequently moving house and school. Her mother's domestic jobs would have offered no stability, and I suspect Ema was constantly looking for better work. Each time she found a job, she would have had to find a nearby room to rent, which may have entailed a school switch for Riya.

Riya has mainly attended private schools, as that is normal in Nepal. Government schools are known for their notoriously unreliable teachers who rarely turn up and lack books and equipment. More than half the schools in Kathmandu are private, and they do not have the prestige that private schools have in Western countries. Most private schools are run on a shoestring and are a necessary alternative to state-run schools.

Ema had enrolled Riya at several Christian schools, but sadly, patriarchy still dominated these. At the age of 12, her male teacher, who was only 18 years old and a student in grade twelve, had sidled up to her on several occasions and made her highly uncomfortable. She had reported this to another teacher, who informed the female principal, but sadly the principal scolded Riya for not telling her first, rather than disciplining the male teacher. Unfortunately, I feel there is a naivety with regard to Christian institutions in Nepal; Christians will implicitly trust any school or orphanage that labels itself as Christian and presume it to be doing good. There is no accountability for them, and I fear harm could occur in much the same way reports of abuse in the Catholic church were ignored for many years.

Ema removed Riya from that school, and she attended several others before entering college for her Plus Two education (equivalent to A-levels). While there, she experienced constant harassment from the boys in her year, who seemed to get away with endless lewd comments without being challenged. On one occasion, she went alone to a classroom at the top of the school's staircase to fetch a book. A boy followed her and closed the classroom door behind them. Riya found out later that he had told her friend, who was waiting at the bottom of the staircase, to go away and leave the two of them alone. Thankfully, despite his threats, her friend ignored the boy and came to find her. This friend was confident and brash, and though Riya is shy herself, she believes God has given her sassy friends who will stand up for and protect her.

At the age of 14, Riya was baptized. Church members dug a pond in their compound and lined it with plastic before filling it with water. Her uncle, the pastor I met earlier, had the privilege of baptizing her. She was glad to be surrounded by family when it took place.

When Riya was 16 years old, a man approached her mother for Riya's hand in marriage. He was 28 years old, an orphan who did not have parents to arrange his marriage. They sensibly refused since Riya was so young, and Riya appears to be quite anti-marriage. She told me that she aimed to take care of her mother by herself; she didn't want a man to do this.

Speaking from her own experience, Ema told Riya, 'Boys can appear nice, but they are often bad.' Saru and I looked at each other at this point in the conversation; we are both mothers of older teenage boys, and we didn't want Riya to think all young men are awful. Of course, Riya shouldn't feel she has to get married, that's up to her, but I hope she can find some good men who can restore the broken image she seems to have of them. It appears that the pain her father's departure caused has left a big scar in this regard.

Riya's face lit up when we talked about church and Bible college. Since she now lives in the same compound as her church, she gets involved in everything, from cleaning to preaching. She told me that everything she does for the church, even washing the floor, helps her feel closer to God. Her heart for serving was evident, and that was why she joined Bible college; she wants to serve God throughout her life.

Bible college sounds like a challenge, though. She attends Nepal Korea International College (NKIC), which can't openly use 'Bible' or 'Christian' in its name as that would provoke opposition from local authorities. Chapel begins at 5 a.m. each day, and if students miss it, they don't get lunch. Each year has around thirty students, and at the time of writing, only the first-year students were attending in-person classes due to Covid. Students in other years were studying from home. Riya lives in a hostel near the college with the other female students, and she told me they looked after their shared quarters well, whereas the boys' hostel was a pigsty.

I've entitled this chapter 'Runners' as I love how Ema has been able to pass her love of God onto Riya, just like a relay runner passes on the baton. Having grown up surrounded by Christians, Riya told me she had always felt close to God and prayed to him all the time. She testified to his love and countless answered prayers; it was evident her faith was strong. She and her mother have faced many hardships but have overcome them through prayer. When Riya faces difficulties now, her family advise her to pray and tell her, 'God has more to do in you.' Consequently, she hopes to work for an organization that helps women in the future, particularly women like her mother.

Riya was studying the well-known Christian book *The Purpose Driven Life* by Rick Warren.[11] In many ways, I think the book's title sums up the main difference between her life and her mother's. Having had faith since she was a child, Riya knows God has good plans for her, and she is on earth for a reason. She revealed that when her mother gave birth to her at the maternity hospital, another couple offered to buy Riya from her. Riya was understandably thankful and proud that her mother refused their deal. I was also relieved and excited that the next generation of Nepali Christian women is so assured of their value and purpose; it's quite a change. I pray Riya will find great delight in everything God has in store for her; women in Nepal need more Christians like her.

Conclusion

Writing this book has been such a privilege from beginning to end. I am overwhelmed by the honesty of the women I have interviewed; they have entrusted their stories to me, and I feel an enormous sense of responsibility to share them. Please, pass on your copy of this book to someone else; don't let their stories stop with you.

The ladies shed many tears during their interviews, but Saru reassures me they were healing tears. Almost every woman expressed appreciation at the end of our conversations; they were grateful that someone had taken the time to hear their stories. Likewise, I wish to thank my readers for making space in your life to learn about women in Nepal.

Heading up WWR means that I hear many horror stories from the women we help, but I don't want to lose the sense of shock and compassion that I had to begin with. My prayer is that I won't become hard-hearted from it all, and I pray that having read this book, you will not either.

Of all the stories I heard during the interview process, the one that has stuck with me the most is Kopisha's experience with her in-laws. They neglected Kopisha's daughter, their granddaughter, to the extent that it led to her death at just 18 months. Kopisha's father-in-law was a Hindu priest and I find it truly appalling that his religious beliefs did not encourage him to care for his granddaughter. I cannot comprehend such evil, and when cultural patriarchal values are this entrenched, it reminds me that 'we are not fighting against flesh-and-blood enemies, but against evil rulers and authorities of the unseen world, against mighty powers in this dark world, and against evil spirits in the heavenly places' (Eph. 6:12).

Two other stories have profoundly influenced me, though perhaps having heard them before, they did not shock me quite as much as Kopisha's (evidence that I need to guard against becoming hard-hearted). One was Suki's description of her experience as the mother of a human trafficking victim. Her isolation and powerlessness during the decade her daughter was missing, and since then, were utterly heartbreaking. Thankfully, human trafficking has garnered a lot of attention in Christian circles over recent years, but most of the focus has been on the victims themselves. Suki's story highlights the need for entire families to receive help and rehabilitation. Suki's sons have shunned their sister, which is a source of great sadness for her. Stigma and the ostracism it induces are potent forces in Nepali society, and as someone from a Western culture, I often fail to understand or appreciate its effect.

The other person who has had a deep impact on me is Maria. Around a decade ago, when I first heard she had been forced to marry her rapist, I was in shock. It was another example of evil in the name of patriarchism. At the time, I began to research other examples of women having to marry their rapists and discovered it is sadly not uncommon. I hope that this research will form the basis of another book; watch this space.

The most fun story to write was Anju's; when I met with her, she told her story with a sparkle in her eye. As a shrewd businesswoman, her experience was different from that of the other women WWR helps, and I am grateful to God for leading me to include her in this book. Her interview came about almost by accident. If anyone was looking to make a movie about a woman in Nepal, I believe her story would be perfect; there were so many ups and downs. She surprised me with everything she had been involved in and the enormous sums she had amassed. Above all, she gave glory to God for everything.

Towards the end of the chapter about Binsa, I updated readers on progress with our efforts to obtain citizenship for Tanya. Sadly, her trip to Solukhumbu with our lawyer fell through. The ward officer in Solukhumbu stated that Tanya also needed to be accompanied by a family member to complete the necessary paperwork. Only a family member from the same ward would do if she was to make any progress. Tanya's helpful aunt, who is willing to assist her, is sadly from a different ward. Only Tanya's adopted mother is from the same ward, but she vehemently refuses to travel to Solukhumbu with Tanya; the enmity between them is very great. I feel so frustrated that Tanya is still waiting to be legally recognized. Our young lawyer has suggested we change tack and apply for Tanya to become a recognized orphan in Lalitpur, where Tanya now lives. Proving that someone is an orphan has its own legal challenges, and I pray that progress for Tanya will be made soon.

Two themes recurred in the stories the women told. One was the power of in-laws and the influence they have over the lives of their daughters-in-law. God cares deeply about relationships, and I believe he wants to redeem the relationship between daughters and mothers-in-law in Nepali culture. I pray for that and invite you to join me.

The other theme that often cropped up was suicide, and again, I know it is not God's will. He longs to comfort those who suffer and feel hopeless. My prayer is for Nepal to be filled with Christians who offer hope and show God's comfort to those considering ending their life.

Unwittingly, I repeatedly mentioned another issue throughout the book, namely Covid. When I wrote in the introduction that the pandemic had already dragged by November 2020, I had no idea that I would still be writing about Covid at the end of the book.

All of the stories in this book are told through the lens of a Christian woman from England. I am not a neutral spectator and have my own biases and experience, from which it is impossible to rid myself. Perhaps I have overemphasized some aspects of the stories, and I am sure I have overlooked other issues. The best way to rectify this is for the women to tell their own stories and write them in their own words. Sadly, most of the women I have included have limited literacy and don't have the power to contact publishers. However, their children have the skills and potential to write and voice their experiences. I will be delighted if a Nepali woman writes the next book about Christians in Nepal.

Ishya asked what I hoped to achieve by sharing these stories. I have many aims. I'd love to encourage more people to take an interest in the lives of Nepali and Asian women in general. I hope that this book has provided plenty of fodder for prayer. As the stories demonstrate, Nepal has many needs, and I hope to stir people to action. Perhaps you could take on the challenge of ending *chaupadi* or become a doctor or nurse specializing in caring for people with leprosy. Both human trafficking and exploitative labour practices need to stop; you can take action to stop these by working in Nepal or by joining an anti-human trafficking organization in your home country. I would be delighted to hear of young people who read this book and decide to orient their lives around making a difference for the women of Nepal and Asia.

Thank you for reading to the end. I am delighted that you have come to Kathmandu with me. As someone who loves to share their experiences with others, it has been devastating for me that, thanks to Covid, no one has been able to visit us while we have been living in Nepal. This book is my way of sharing my passion for the country with others, and I'd love to speak with anyone who wants to learn more. Please let me know whose stories have touched you, and if you can find a way to visit Nepal, I hope you do so. Apart from any other impact you might make, the country is hugely reliant on tourist income; simply by coming to Nepal and spending money, you'll provide jobs and sustain the economy. I hope and pray that Nepal and its women have found a place in your heart; please keep praying for them.

A Prayer for Nepal

Inspired by Psalm 72 and Isaiah 40

Father God, we praise you for creating the beautiful country of Nepal. The majestic mountains attest to your glory, and the rushing rivers and waterfalls remind us of your overflowing goodness.

Lord, we confess that we have not always been aware of the trials and difficulties that the people of Nepal have to endure. We have been ignorant of the hardships Nepal's women face and ask you to help us remember them. You see their troubles and never look away or forget; your understanding is immeasurable.

Thank you for promising to rescue the poor when they cry out to you and for helping the oppressed who have no one else to defend them. We are grateful that you are a God of compassion who feels pity for the weak and needy.

Almighty God, we ask you to save Nepal's precious women from all oppression and violence. We ask you to give power to Nepali women who are tired and worn out. May those who are ill-treated be given strength. Please speak your words of comfort to them, and may they hear them clearly during their times of loneliness and isolation. Thank you for speaking tenderly to them.

We ask you to continue defending the poor and rescuing the children of the needy. Though the nation of Nepal is disadvantaged in so many ways, we pray that there will be prosperity for all and that the hills and mountains will be fruitful. Please bring rains to refresh the fields, and may the godly flourish.

Guide us, Lord, and teach us how best to respond to the needs of Nepal's people. Please help us uphold justice for them and treat the poor fairly. When judgement is required, please give us wisdom. Inspire us to defend and rescue those who struggle. When we do this successfully, may all the glory go to you.

We hold onto your promise that those who wait on the Lord will fly high on wings like eagles and run and not grow faint. We eagerly anticipate many more testimonies to the saving work you are doing in Nepal.

Amen

How to Help

Women Without Roofs – Nepal
www.wwr-nepal.org

The organization Anna set up and continues to help run. It supports vulnerable women, including those described in this book (with the exception of Saru), by contributing towards their rent, medical bills and children's education.

Women are referred to WWR by a committed team of pastors and their wives or by women we are already helping. The women we aid do not have to be Christian for us to help them.

Esther and Nina arrange to meet the new woman in her home to assess her circumstances. They ensure she is on her own and doesn't have other sources of income she may not have told her pastor about. If the woman meets our criteria, we begin contributing towards her rent and any medical bills immediately. Esther and Nina will also ask about the woman's children, and if they are of school age or younger, WWR will provide a fixed sum per month per child.

Usually, these grants are sufficient to get a woman back on her feet. She knows we are with her for the long-term and can find security knowing she won't be thrown out of her home for lack of rent money. She will still need to work to buy food and clothes for herself and her children, but this gives her a reason to get up in the morning and improves mental health.

Some women are now too old to work, and they receive a small subsistence grant from WWR to help pay for food and other essentials. Furthermore, those women who cannot live independently due to old age, ill-health or mental health issues are invited to live at our women's home, Mahima Griha. At the women's home, all meals and accommodation are provided free of charge and the women receive a small stipend to pay for extras.

WWR tries to help the ladies with other issues, as mentioned in the book. Recently we have employed a lawyer to assist with obtaining citizenship. We have also worked with other organizations to provide training and education on various topics, including first aid, handicrafts and health.

The following organizations do fantastic work in Nepal. They have actively assisted us in improving the welfare of the women we help.

International Nepal Fellowship
www.inf.org

Partnering with local organizations, INF serves Nepal's poorest and most remote communities.

Kevin Rohan Memorial Ecological Foundation
www.krmef.com

KRMEF's goal is to create and implement eco-friendly programmes designed to promote and encourage sustainable community development.

Koshish

www.koshishnepal.org

Mental self-help organization. Established in 2008, Koshish, a National Mental Health Organization, promotes mental health and psychosocial well-being in Nepal. Koshish promotes self-advocacy in the spirit of 'Nothing About Us Without Us'.

Legal Aid and Consultancy Centre

www.laccnepal.org

LACC is a pioneer in providing free legal aid to victims of gender-based violence and human trafficking. It actively promotes women's access to justice.

Maiti Nepal

www.maitinepal.org

Maiti Nepal was born out of a crusade to protect Nepali girls and women from crimes like domestic violence, trafficking for flesh trade, child prostitution, child labour and various forms of abuse, exploitation and torture.

Nepal Leprosy Trust

www.nlt.org.uk

A UK-based Christian agency that provides services to people affected by leprosy in Nepal. They have built and now operate the only major leprosy services centre in south-east Nepal, the area of the country with the highest prevalence of leprosy. Eileen Lodge also established NLT.

Next Generation Nepal

www.nextgenerationnepal.org

At Next Generation Nepal, they reconnect trafficked Nepali children with their families. Taken from rural villages, and at a young age, many of these children end up in illegal orphanages and homes. Often, they are found on the brink of starvation and in terrible conditions. With child trafficking still a significant problem in Nepal, they need your help as much as ever.

Safetyknot

www.safetyknot.org

They keep your family safe. Did you know that every year 90 per cent of the 5 million deaths that occur from injuries happen in a low- or middle-income country? This is why Safetyknot exists. They are here to help keep you safe. They know that keeping your family or organization safe in some countries can be challenging. Their safety resources and training provide you with the safety support you need to keep your family and workforce safe.

The Leprosy Mission

www.leprosymission.org

They are working to defeat leprosy across the world. Leprosy is the leading cause of preventable disability in the world. Around 200,000 people are diagnosed with leprosy every year, and 2–3 million live with leprosy-related disabilities. The Leprosy Mission supports Anandaban Hospital.

The Washing Machine Project
www.thewashingmachineproject.org

At The Washing Machine Project, it's their mission to alleviate the burden of hand-washing clothes for everyone, everywhere.

United Mission to Nepal
www.umn.org.np

United Mission to Nepal (UMN) strives to address the root causes of poverty as it serves the people of Nepal in the name and spirit of Jesus Christ. Established in 1954, UMN is a cooperative effort between the people of Nepal and a large number of Christian organizations from nearly twenty countries on four continents.

Acknowledgements

God has graciously surrounded me with supportive friends, family and colleagues. I am indebted to them for their help and encouragement as I have written this book.

Esther has faithfully managed WWR in Nepal since 2005; the high regard that the women have for her has enabled me to interview them. Her honesty, compassion and faith have made WWR the success it is, and none of our activities would be possible without her. At the start of this book, she patiently translated for me and has always been generous with her time and knowledge of Nepal.

Saru became my translator during later chapters and generously shared her story in Chapter 6. As a pastor's wife, she showed deep and spiritual compassion for the ladies we met with and created a safe environment for them to open up to me. While writing up their stories, I sent many questions to her via WhatsApp, and she good-naturedly responded to them all. I am hugely grateful.

The staff at Authentic Media have been so encouraging, and I'm thankful for their belief in me and this book. Knowing that they pray for their authors is tremendously reassuring.

While quarantining in the UK in late 2020, Andy and Phil allowed me to shut myself away in their annexe, where I wrote the opening chapters. It was a beautiful space to write in, and their generosity made the writing process a true pleasure. Thank you for enabling a brilliant beginning for the book.

My friend Sue spoke a word of encouragement to me just when I needed to hear it. Perhaps she won't remember what she said, but it was a gift to me. Your care for Zach and Beth has made a huge difference, too; living in Nepal has many challenges, and knowing they have you and your family nearby is a great comfort.

As I entered the final straight of the writing process, Lorna showed great enthusiasm for one of the chapters, which helped me cross the finish line. She was the most ardent advocate for my last book, and I am thankful for her.

A faithful group of trustees oversees WWR. Nic, Jan and Marilyn share their wisdom and remain committed to seeing women's lives in Nepal change for the better. Jess is a steadfast representative for us in the US, and I am so grateful for her assistance and words of encouragement.

WWR exists thanks to the generosity of its sponsors and donors. The impact you have is beyond words and will last for eternity. Thank you.

When I moved to Alabama in 2018, I was at rather a loss to understand why God had sent us there. However, I met the most incredible person whose friendship has been an anchor throughout the writing of this book and the turmoil Covid has inflicted on our family. While praying with her over Zoom, I had a breakthrough in understanding Tanya's story. Jenn, you are a gift from God. Thank you for your words of spiritual comfort and encouragement; I hope it is not too long before we see each other in the real world; I owe you a huge hug.

For two busy teenagers, my children Zach and Beth have shown surprising willingness to read each of the chapters as

I've finished them. I won't reveal which of them hides in the toilet at boarding school so they can read in peace! It has been a privilege to share these stories with you both. I am confident you will continue to be kind and sensitive people who stand up for women.

None of my work would be possible without my husband and the crazy life we lead, thanks to the British Army. So far, we've lived in eighteen houses together, and I suspect there may be several more to come. I know I'm not the easiest person to live with, in particular when I'm immersed in a story of trauma, but you always help lighten my mood and find ways for me to take time out. Thank you for allowing me to follow God's calling to establish WWR and write this book.

Bibliography

Baumann, S. *Assessing the Role of Caste/Ethnicity in Predicting Menstrual Knowledge, Attitudes, and Practices in Nepal* (Pittsburgh, PA: Global Public Health, 2019)

Dix, S. *Corruption and Anti-Corruption in Nepal* (Oslo: Norad, 2011)

Enslin, E. *While the Gods Were Sleeping: A Journey Through Love and Rebellion in Nepal* (Berkeley, CA: Seal Press, 2014)

Gellner, D. *Caste, Ethnicity and Inequality in Nepal* (Mumbai: Sameeksha Trust, 2007)

Gellner, D., S. Hausner, and C. Letizia. *Religion, Secularism, and Ethnicity in Contemporary Nepal* (New Delhi: OUP, 2016)

Gellner, D., and C. Letizia. 'Hinduism in the Secular Republic of Nepal'. Pages 275–304 in *The Oxford History of Hinduism: Modern Hinduism* (ed. T. Brekke; Delhi: OUP, 2019)

General Federation of Nepalese Trade Unions, *Labour Under the Chimney: A Study on the Brick Kilns of Nepal* (Kathmandu: GEFONT, 2007)

Grennan, C. *Little Princes: One Man's Promise to Bring Home the Lost Children of Nepal* (London: HarperCollins, 2011)

Hendry, S. *Radhika's Story: Surviving Human Trafficking* (London: New Holland, 2010)

Human Rights Watch, *No Law, No Justice, No State for Victims: The Culture of Impunity in Post-conflict Nepal* (New York: HRW, 2020)

Hunkins, A. *Voices in the Dark: A Century of Classic Nepali Short Stories About Women* (Kathmandu: Vajra Books, 2017)

Jha, P. *Battles of the New Republic: A Contemporary History of Nepal* (London: Hurst & Company, 2014)

Joshi, V. 'The Birth of Christian Enthusiasm Among the Angami of Nagaland in South Asia', *Journal of South Asian Studies* Vol. XXX, No. 3 (2007): pp. 541–557

Khalid, S., and G. Adhikari. *Nepal: The Maoist Dream: The Story of Civil War Through the Eyes of the Nepali People* (Doha: Al Jazeera, 2016)

King, M., and T. Bielak. 'Impaired Episodic Memory for Events Encoded During Mania in Patients with Bipolar Disorder'. *Psychiatry Research*, 25 (2013): pp. 213–219

Liechty, M. *Suitably Modern: Making Middle-Class Culture in a New Consumer Society* (Princeton, NJ: Princeton University Press, 2002)

Limbu, A. *Trafficking and Forced Labour in Nepal: A Review of the Literature* (Kathmandu: Himal Books, 2011)

Lovera, J., and M. Punaks, *Reintegration Guidelines for Trafficked and Displaced Children Living in Institutions* (Eugene, OR: Next Generation Nepal, 2015)

Nepal Leprosy Trust, *A Touch of Providence: The Story of Nepal Leprosy Trust* (London: NLT, 2018)

Nimri Aziz, B. *Yogmaya & Durga Devi: Rebel Women of Nepal* (Kathmandu: Mandala Book Point, 2020)

Olson, C.G. *What in the World Is God Doing* (Cedar Knolls, NJ: Global Gospel Publishers, 2003)

Rana, S. *Singha Durbar: Rise and Fall of the Rana Regime of Nepal* (New Delhi: Rupa, 2017)

Reed, N. *My Seventh Monsoon: A Himalayan Journey of Faith and Mission* (Milton Keynes: Authentic Media, 2011)

Sanjel S., S.N. Khanal, S.M. Thygerson, K. Khanal, Z. Pun, S. Tamang, and S.K. Joshi. 'Airborne Particulate Matter and Health Condition in Brick Kiln Workers in Kathmandu Valley, Nepal', *Kathmandu University Medical Journal*, Vol. 14, No. 2, Issue 54 (2016): pp. 159–166

Shrestha, T. *From Exclusion to Inclusion of Nepali Women: A Myth or Reality?* (Kathmandu: INSEC, 2009)

Simpson, C. *The Girl from Kathmandu: Twelve Dead Men and a Woman's Quest for Justice* (New York: HarperCollins, 2018)

Suji, M. *A Country of Minorities* (New Delhi: Books for Change, 2016)

Tambs-Lyche, H. 'Caste: History and the Present', *Academia Letters* 1311 (2021)

Thapa, D. *Day of the Maoist* (Colombo: Himal Southasian, 2001)

Timsina, N.R. *Trend of Urban Growth in Nepal With a Focus in Kathmandu Valley: A Review of Processes and Drivers of Change* (Edinburgh: Urban Risk Hub, 2020)

Upadhyay, S. *Arresting God in Kathmandu* (New Delhi: Rupa, 2001)

Upadhyay, S. *The Royal Ghosts* (New Delhi: Rupa, 2006)

Wagle, N. *Palpasa Café* (Kathmandu: Publication Nepalaya, 2018)

Warren, R. *The Purpose Driven Life* (Grand Rapids, MI: Zondervan, 2002)

Wickeri, E. '"Land is Life, Land is Power": Landlessness, Exclusion, and Deprivation in Nepal', *Fordham International Law Journal*, Vol. 34, Issue 4 (2011): pp. 930–1040

Further Resources

Filmography

I am Belmaya, distributed by Tideturner Films

Mimi distributed by Jio Cinema

Stories by Rabindranath Tagore distributed by EPIC India

Websites

About The Leprosy Mission Nepal https://tlmnepal.org/tlmnepal/#about-us (accessed 13 December 2020)

International Textbook of Leprosy https://www.internationaltextbookofleprosy.org/ (accessed 14 December 2020)

Maiti Nepal https://maitinepal.org/ (accessed 24 September 2021)

Menstruation and human rights – Frequently asked questions, United Nations Population Fund https://www.unfpa.org/menstruationfaq (accessed 15 January 2020)

'Migrant workers in Brick Kilns of Kathmandu Valley', https://aawaajnews.com/social-news/migrant-workers-in-brick-kilns-of-kathmandu-valley/ (accessed 12 January 2022)

'Nepal: Reports of Maoist rebel activity in the Solukhumbu district; whether the Maoists commit abuses against the ethnic Sherpa living there; whether the Maoists have extorted money from Sherpas and owners of trekking lodges in the Solukhumbu district (2001-2003)' https://www.refworld.org/docid/3f7d4de818.html (accessed 11 October 2021)

Operation World, Nepal, InterVarsity Press https://www.operationworld.org/country/nepa/owtext.html (accessed 5 December 2020)

'People visit hospitals in the night for COVID-19 tests to avoid social stigma' https://myrepublica.nagariknetwork.com/news/people-visit-hospitals-in-the-night-for-covid-19-tests-to-avoid-social-stigma/ (accessed 16 June 2021)

'Schools Shut Till January 29' https://thehimalayantimes.com/nepal/schools-shut-till-january-29 (accessed 11 January 2022)

Shanta Bhawan: Palace of Peace http://ecs.com.np/features/shanta-bhawan-palace-of-peace (accessed 15 December 2020)

'Taboos Undercut Nepal's Marital Rape Law' https://womensenews.org/2012/01/taboos-undercut-nepals-marital-rape-law/ (accessed 17 April 2021)

'Ten most consumed things during *Dashain* festival' https://english.nepalpress.com/2021/10/12/10-most-consumed-things-during-dashain-festival (accessed 9 November 2021)

'The Last Headhunters of Nagaland' https://thediplomat.com/2018/04/the-last-headhunters-of-nagaland/ (accessed 2 February 2022)

'Throat Cancer Causes & Risk Factors' https://www.mskcc.org/cancer-care/types/throat/throat-cancer-risk-factors-prevention (accessed 12 October 2021)

'Women and Water' https://www.nepalitimes.com/editorial/women-and-water/ (accessed 13 November 2021)

'Women Under 40 Require a Letter, and Permission From Family to Travel Abroad' https://myrepublica.nagariknetwork.com/news/women-under-40-require-a-letter-to-travel-abroad-doi-director-paudel/#/ (accessed 14 April 2021)

Notes

1 Hyacinth Bucket was a character in the BBC television show *Keeping Up Appearances*. She was known for organizing everyone and wanting to appear 'posh'.

2 'This is the Day', paraphrased by Les Garrett, St. 1 © 1967, 1980, Scripture in Song. Admin by Integrity Music.

3 Nepalis call their cousins 'brother' and 'sister'.

4 The Indian Army calls their Nepali soldiers 'Gorkhas' and the British Army refers to them as 'Gurkhas'.

5 Naomi Reed, *My Seventh Monsoon: A Himalayan Journey of Faith and Mission* (Milton Keynes: Authentic Media, 2011), p. 44.

6 Elizabeth Enslin, *While the Gods Were Sleeping: A Journey Through Love and Rebellion in Nepal* (Berkeley, CA: Seal Press, 2014).

7 In Nepal, marriage ceremonies may or may not occur, depending on whether the family can afford one. Other than 'husband', there is no term for a woman to refer to a man she lives with. Very modern women might use the English word 'boyfriend', but this is fairly scandalous for ordinary women.

8 Memorial Sloan Kettering Cancer Centre, 'Throat Cancer Causes & Risk Factors', https://www.mskcc.org/cancer-care/types/throat/throat-cancer-risk-factors-prevention (accessed 12 October 2021).

9 General Federation of Nepalese Trade Unions, *Labour Under the Chimney: A Study on the Brick Kilns of Nepal* (Kathmandu: GEFONT, 2007).

10 C.G. Olson, *What in the World Is God Doing* (Cedar Knolls, NJ: Global Gospel Publishers, 2003).

11 Rick Warren, *The Purpose Driven Life* (Grand Rapids, MI: Zondervan, 2002).

Authentic

We trust you enjoyed reading this book from Authentic. If you want to be informed of any new titles from this author and other releases you can sign up to the Authentic newsletter by scanning below:

Online:
authenticmedia.co.uk

Follow us: